Round About a Great Estate

'The beautiful light came through the elms of the rickyard, away from the ridge of the distant Down, and then for the first hour of the day the room was aglow. For quite two hundred years every visible sunrise had shone in at that window more or less, as the season changed and the sun rose to the north of east. Perhaps it was that sense of ancient homeliness that caused Cicely, without knowing why, to steal in there alone to dream, for nowhere else indoors could she have been so far away from the world of to-day.'

From Chapter II, page 28

Cicely

ROUND ABOUT A GREAT ESTATE

Richard Jefferies

Introduction and Glossary by John Fowles

Illustrations by Graham Arnold

Ex Libris Press

In co-operation with the Richard Jefferies Society

First published 1880
This edition published 1987 by
Ex Libris Press
1 The Shambles
Bradford on Avon
Wiltshire

Cover by 46 Design, Bradford on Avon
Typeset in 11 on 13 point Baskerville by
Saxon Printing Ltd., Derby

Printed in Great Britain by A. Wheaton & Co. Ltd, Exeter

ISBN 0 948578 10 6

CONTENTS

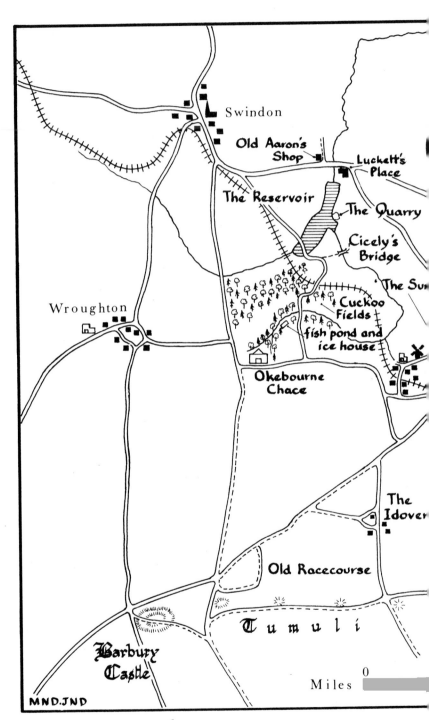

Swindon

Old Aaron's Shop

Luckett's Place

The Reservoir

The Quarry

Cicely's Bridge

'The Sun

Cuckoo Fields

fish pond and ice house

Wroughton

Okebourne Chace

The Idover

Old Racecourse

Tumuli

Barbury Castle

Miles 0

MND.JND

6

The World of Round about a Great Estate

ROUND ABOUT A GREAT ESTATE

BY

RICHARD JEFFERIES

AUTHOR OF
'THE GAMEKEEPER AT HOME' 'WILD LIFE IN A SOUTHERN COUNTY'
'THE AMATEUR POACHER' 'GREENE FERNE FARM'
'HODGE AND HIS MASTERS'

LONDON

SMITH, ELDER, & CO., 15 WATERLOO PLACE

1880

8   *Title page of first edition*

INTRODUCTION

There is, to my mind, only one thing wrong with this book, and that is its title. Jefferies usually managed to find a telling or at least a memorable phrase. Very well, *Round About a Great Estate* is loosely true; but only in a dossier, a file-tab sense. I suspect it is one of the reasons that a new edition has been long overdue, and why it has seemingly been the least read of its kind.

Whatever the reason, it is a great pity. This is both the lightest and the richest, and easily the most attractive (as stern a critic as Mrs Leavis pronounced it 'one of the most delightful books in the English language') of Jefferies' output in what we may call (with some trepidation - can so short a life have periods?) his second period. It comes from the heart of his special landscape, in every sense: personally, historically, spiritually, aesthetically. A few years ago an American friend, and lover of Thoreau, demanded to know what he should read of this obscure Englishman that I had the impudence to compare with his own great idol. At the time I gave him other titles. I was a fool, I should have mentioned this one book alone. If it does not hook the sceptical trout, nothing else will.

Round About a Great Estate was first published in 1880, at first as a serial in the *Pall Mall Gazette* , then by Smith, Elder and Co. in a soberly pretty little volume with a blue and gilt binding, that bore on its front, as also on its title-page, the cut of a wood anemone leaf that Jefferies himself had made. It belongs to, and concludes, that quartet of books of linked essays, made up of *The Gamekeeper at Home* (1878), *Wild Life in a Southern County* and *The Amateur Poacher* (both 1879); in a very fertile period which also saw the publication in 1880 of *Hodge and His Masters* and the novel *Green Ferne Farm*. It was a period where one feels that Jefferies was most at peace with himself. He had discovered where his world was, where his skills lay, since his thirtieth birthday in 1878. He was no longer the dreamy young fellow ('moony Dick') and vague disgrace ('a lazy loppet') to his family. The best of his novels and his masterpiece, *The Story of My Heart,* still lay ahead, as did also the ill-health and suffering that were to kill him finally in 1887 - though in the latter case only just ahead, since the first attack of fistulae came at the end of 1881. But the shadow of death was not yet on him in 1880. This is a happy book.

Jefferies had left his birthplace for the London suburb of Surbiton early in 1877, and it seems, as with so many writers, that he almost needed this 'exile' to return artistically to his roots. The experts, those seekers after simple answers, differ a little as to the autobiographical links that may be made. The estate in question, 'Okebourne Chace', is almost certainly that of Burderop Park, just south of Swindon, while 'Okebourne Village' is Chiseldon on the map. The Lucketts' farm seems clearly Jefferies' own previous home, the small farm at Coate (it was never the true Coate Farm of the maps), on the Swindon side of the same estate, which had been sold in 1878. But some think it was partly modelled on his father-in-law's, Daye House Farm in the parish of Chiseldon, as Hilary Luckett himself on that father-in-law, Andrew Baden. Yet here the evidence is strongly for the original being Jefferies' own father, James Luckett Jefferies. It is certainly a somewhat idealized portrait; of the father Jefferies might have wished himself, rather than of the real man, who we know had mixed feelings about his property, and was hardly a success there. However, we have it on the real man's own evidence that he visited his son in Surbiton in 1877 (when he first put the farm on sale) and gave him a great deal of information about both family and local past.

The name Luckett had entered the family when a great-grandfather, also Richard Jefferies, had married a Frances Luckett of Lechlade. Mrs Luckett in the book seems likewise to have been a portrait (again, idealized) of his mother. Edward Thomas's 'sun-sweet shadow of a character', Cicely, was no doubt based in part on his wife Jessie (they had married in 1874), and perhaps also on Molly, a real milkmaid on his father's farm; yet she is equally certainly in part a psychological and temperamental mask for Jefferies himself, as was Felise in *The Dewy Morn* and Amaryllis in the last novel he published. *Amaryllis at the Fair* (1887) contains a much less idealized view of Jefferies and his close family (there called the Idens) and one may see it as a fully fictionalized yet more honest version of the Luckett part of the present book.

Several other characters in *Round About a Great Estate* may be traced to real 'characters' (in the colloquial sense) at Coate. Old Aaron was Job Brown, both wicked poacher and keeper of a village shop there; while young Aaron was drawn from one of the farm workmen, probably Abner Webb, who was notorious for his drinking. Old farmer Jonathan of The Idovers (Draycot Foliat, a Chiseldon hamlet, in reality) harks back to an eighteenth century John Jefferies who farmed there, and founded both the Draycot and the Swindon branches of the family.

We may leave such learned biographical deciphering to the experts. It is at least clear that in this book Jefferies, newly confident both of his potential market and his technique, wanted to combine several different aims: one, as always, was to express his deep love of his native countryside and its wild life, in the now; but he also wanted to say something of his own yeoman roots in it, and beyond that, something of its past and present life in what today we would call sociological and cultural terms - that is, its human side. In this last he was to a certain extent retreating into his own tyro period, to the time in the late 1860s when he had grown local historian from local journalist. It is not strictly an autobiographical book; yet it has a very personal, family atmosphere, which distinguishes it from the three other works of the quartet.

There were always two selves in Jefferies. One is the good journalist, the gifted reporter of what he sees; another a much more secret person, aware that he is unable by such objective means to express what he really feels, really *is*. He was never a born novelist, like Hardy, instinctively at home in the form; yet I believe he persisted with it (or as here, with quasi-fictional treatment) because it allowed him to express so many inner and subjective feelings that the 'good reporter' self denied. This is already evident in the novel of 1880, *Greene Ferne Farm*, and *Round About a Great Estate* marks a clear transition from that good reporter self to the much deeper full personality, whose apotheosis came in *Bevis, The Story* and *Amaryllis at the Fair*.

But where *Round About a Great Estate* excels is in the style that

Jefferies evolved to modulate between his two selves. Edward Thomas was, I think, being less than kind when he described that style as 'effortless and in places slipshod', and conveying 'a careless acceptance of things as they are'; rather as if it were merely tossed out to please a publisher and a growing audience. It seems to me much more an outstanding example of a haphazard yet cunning simplicity, and in some ways as remarkable for what it does not say as for what it does. Hilary Luckett remarks at the very end that God made nothing tidy, to explain why he does not like seeing the trees and shrubs in the farm garden closely pruned. Jefferies' method in the book closely echoes this. His prose is like nature itself. It may seem highly inconsequential, like a country amble, largely made up of whims, of following one's nose, grasshoppering from one mood or subject to the next. It is only at the end that more sensitive readers will recognize they have just been gently - if sometimes quirkily - led through a miracle of casual-seeming simplicity into matters and feelings far beyond any one small local landscape.

The accuracy of Jefferies' observations will please any modern naturalist: here we are - and still today - being taught to see. Yet what is striking is the lightness of the teaching, how free it is of any modern scientific approach; no Latin names, though plenty of local dialect ones; no reification, no mechanical explanation of phenomena, no quotations from more learned texts. He briefly mentions in one place two kinds of oak-gall, the oak-apple and the knopper; yet not a mention of the parasitic wasps that produce them, the kind of thing any modern writer would feel obliged to include. The book appeared at the very beginning of the revolution in nature-study - and natural science - usually dated to the Education Act of 1870, exemplified in Thomas Huxley, and associated with German science: that stern demand for ever greater technical knowledge (and jargon), and not only in its professional students, but in all who pretended to be interested in nature. We still suffer from the consequences of that huge cultural rift. It has left us on the one hand with all those amateurs who are in everything but name professional scientists, and on the other with the purple-prose sentimentalists - two unattractive extremes that have in general disillusioned ordinary nature-lovers far more than nature itself. Only Ruskin opposed this invasion of science at the beginning, and roundly declared it inimical to art, and subversive of our capacity to benefit from nature emotionally.

Jefferies is an admirable proof of Ruskin's view, and especially in this book. Modern naturalists may now know far more of the workings of nature than Jefferies; but there are countless places here where we can see that in his heart he remains far closer to it than they. They know nature: he felt it, with all his being. And the same is true in that other important matter of the book, Jefferies' account of the agricultural and rural transition between the first and third quarters of the last century. That too will not pass as serious, scientific history, studded with wheat-price graphs and emigration statistics. Yet for all its anecdotes, its personal touches, its family memories, it works brilliantly well, because it is essentially a human, and humane, view. Jefferies himself, as he makes clear in his preface (and in countless other places), was no would-be Luddite, with his face turned firmly backwards. What he wants is progress, but progress in a natural light, not in a sun 'timed by the clock'.

At first sight there may seem to us something of a nostalgic melancholy over the memories he gathered of the past: the speed with which things pass, with which society changes, the losses ... in history least of all is God tidy. But here perhaps his book itself is a consolation. In it a past present stays as fresh as the day it was written; indeed so much has changed since Jefferies died that it may risk appearing now as sentimentally idyllic. All his life one of his favourite authors was the Homer of the *Odyssey,* and something of that Homer has always lain for me in the quieter passages of *Round About a Great Estate,* indeed more there than in the obvious parallels, like the one about village fighting. Such a passage begins Chapter VIII. I have always loved it, with its celebration, both precise and generalized, of an ancient world and its simplicities. It is a poem, though not in verse; and one worthy of William Barnes or John Clare.

These glimpses, moods, evocations of a garden of Eden almost beyond imagining in our own neurotic and bedevilled century are one major reason why we keep reading Jefferies. But that we should think of them as 'sentimentally' idyllic says far less of the writer's intention than of our own lack of innocence, of capacity for feeling. It certainly betrays our ignorance of Jefferies himself. He was categorically not a sentimentalist, either over nature or rural reality, and much else besides.

What he stood for ... but let him speak now. He best will let you know what he was, and remains.

John Fowles, 1986.

PREFACE

There is an old story which in respect of a modern application may bear re-telling. Once upon a time in a lonely 'coombe-bottom' of the Downs, where there was neither church, chapel, nor public building of any kind, there lived a cottage-girl who had never seen anything of civilisation. A friend, however, having gone out to service in a market-town some few miles distant, she one day walked in to see her, and was shown the wonders of the place, the railway, the post-office, the hotels, and so forth. In the evening the friend accompanied her a short way on the return journey, and as they went out of the town, they passed the church. Looking suddenly up at the tower, the visitor exclaimed, 'Lard-a-mussy! you've got another moon here. Yourn have got figures all round un!' In her excitement, and prepared to see marvels, she had mistaken the large dial of the church clock for a moon of a different kind to the one which shone upon her native home. This old tale, familiar to country folk as an illustration of simplicity, has to-day a wider meaning. Until recent years the population dwelling in villages and hamlets, and even in little rural towns, saw indeed the sun by day and the moon by night, and learned the traditions and customs of their forefathers, such as had been handed down for generations. But now a new illumination has fallen upon these far-away places. The cottager is no longer ignorant, and his child is well grounded in rudimentary education, reads and writes with facility, and is not without knowledge of the higher sort. Thus there is now another moon with the figures of education all round it. In this book some notes have been made of the former state of things before it passes away entirely. But I would not have it therefore thought that I wish it to continue or return. My sympathies and hopes are with the light of the future, only I should like it to come from nature. The clock should be read by the sunshine, not the sun timed by the clock. The latter is indeed impossible, for though all the clocks in the world should declare the hour of dawn to be midnight, the sun will presently rise just the same.

Richard Jefferies

Chapter 1

Okebourne Chace.   Felling Trees.

The great house at Okebourne Chace stands in the midst of the park, and from the southern windows no dwellings are visible. Near at hand the trees appear isolated, but further away insensibly gather together, and above them rises the distant Down crowned with four tumuli. Among several private paths which traverse the park there is one that, passing through a belt of ash wood, enters the meadows. Sometimes following the hedges and sometimes crossing the angles, this path finally ends, after about a mile, in the garden surrounding a large thatched farmhouse. In the maps of the parish it has probably another name, but from being so long inhabited by the Lucketts it is always spoken of as Lucketts' Place.

The house itself and ninety acres of grass land have been their freehold for many generations; in fact, although there is no actual deed of entail, the property is as strictly preserved in the family and descends from heir to heir as regularly as the great estate and mansion adjacent. Old Hilary Luckett – though familiarly called 'old', he is physically in the prime of life – is probably about the most independent man in the county. Yet he is on terms of more than goodwill with the great house, and rents one of the largest farms on the estate, somewhere between six and seven hundred acres. He has the right of shooting, and in the course of years privilege after privilege has been granted, till Hilary is now as free of the warren as the owner of the charter himself. If you should be visiting Okebourne Chace, and any question should arise whether of horses, dog, or gun, you are sure to be referred to Hilary. Hilary knows all about it: he is the authority thereabout on all matters concerning game. Is it proposed to plant fresh covers? Hilary's opinion is asked. Is it proposed to thin out some of the older trees; what does Hilary say?

It is a fact that people really believe no part of a partridge is ever taken away after being set before him. Neither bones nor sinews remain: so fond is he of the brown bird. Having eaten the breast, and the juicy leg and the delicate wing, he next proceeds to suck the bones; for game to be thoroughly enjoyed should be eaten like a mince-pie, in the fingers. There is always one bone with a sweeter flavour than the rest, just at the joint or fracture: it varies in every bird according to the chance of the cooking, but, having discovered it, put it aside for further and more strict attention. Presently he begins to grind up the bones in his strong teeth, commencing with the smallest. His teeth are not now so powerful as when in younger days he used to lift a sack of wheat with them, or the full milking-bucket up to the level of the copper in the dairy. Still they gradually reduce the slender skeleton. The feat is not so difficult if the bird has been well hung.

He has the right to shoot, and need take no precautions. But, in fact, a farmer, whether he has liberty or not, can usually amuse himself occasionally in that way. If his labourer sees him quietly slipping up beside the hedge with his double-barrel towards the copse in the corner where a pheasant has been heard several times lately, the labourer watches him with delight, and says nothing. Should anyone in authority ask where that gun went off, the labourer 'thenks it wur th'birdkippur up in th'Dree Vurlong, you.' Presently the pheasant hangs in the farmer's cellar, his long tail sweeping the top of the XXX cask; and the 'servant-wench', who is in and out all day, also says nothing. Nor can anything exceed the care with which she disposes of the feathers when she picks the bird. There is a thorough sympathy between master and man so far. Hilary himself, with all that great estate to sport over, cannot at times refrain from stepping across the boundary. His landlord once, it is whispered, was out with Hilary shooting, and they became so absent-minded while discussing some interesting subject as to wander several fields beyond the property before they discovered their mistake.

At Lucketts' Place the favourite partridge always comes up for supper: a pleasant meal that nowadays can rarely be had out of a farmhouse. Then the bright light from the burning log outshines the lamp, and glances rosy on the silver tankard standing under a glass shade on a bracket against the wall. Hilary's father won it near half a century since in some heats that were run on the Downs on the old racecourse, before it was ploughed up. For the wicked turnip is responsible for the destruction of old England; far more so than the steam-engine.

Waste lands all glorious with golden blossoming furze, with purple foxglove, or curious orchis hiding in stray corners; wild moor-like lands, beautiful with heaths and honey-bottle; grand stretches of sloping downs where the hares hid in the grass, and where all the horses in the kingdom might gallop at their will; these have been overthrown with the plough because of the turnip. As the root crops came in, the rage began for thinning the hedges and grubbing the double mounds and killing the young timber, besides putting in the drains and driving away the wild-ducks. The wicked turnip put diamonds on the fingers of the farmer's wife, and presently raised his rent. But now some of the land is getting 'turnip-sick', the roots come stringy and small and useless, so that many let it 'vall down'.

After the last crop it is left alone, the couch grows, the docks spread out from the hedges, every species of weed starts up, till by-and-by the ploughed land becomes green and is called pasture. This is a process going on at the present moment, and to which owners of land should see without delay. Hilary has been looked on somewhat coldly by other tenants for openly calling the lord of the manor's attention to it. He sturdily maintains that arable land if laid down for pasture should be laid down properly – a thing that requires labour and expenditure just the same as other farming operations. So the silver tankard, won when 'cups' were not so common as now, is a memorial of the old times before the plough turned up the sweet turf of the racecourse.

Hilary does not bet beyond the modest 'fiver' which a man would be thought unsociable if he did not risk on the horse that carries the country's colours. But he is very 'thick' with the racing-people on the Downs, and supplies the stable with oats, which is, I believe, not an unprofitable commission. The historical anecdote of the Roman emperor who fed his horse on gilded oats reads a little strange when we first come across it in youth. But many a race-horse owner has found reason since to doubt if it be so wonderful, as his own stud – to judge by the cost – must live on golden fodder. Now, before I found this out about the stable, it happened one spring day that I

19

met Hilary in the fields, and listened to a long tirade which he delivered against 'wuts'.

The wheat was then showing a beautiful flag, the despised oats were coming out in jag, and the black knots on the delicate barley straw were beginning to be topped with the hail. The flag is the long narrow green leaf of the wheat; in jag means the spray-like drooping awn of the oat; and the hail is the beard of the barley, which when it is white and brittle in harvest-time gets down the back of the neck, irritating the skin of those who work among it. According to Hilary, oats do not flourish on rich land; and when he was young (and everything was then done right) a farmer who grew oats was looked upon with contempt, as they were thought only fit for the poorest soil, and a crop that therefore denoted poverty. But nowadays, thundered Hilary in scorn, all farmers grow oats, and, indeed, anything in preference to wheat.

Afterwards, at the Derby that year, methought I saw Hilary as I passed the sign of the 'Carrion Crow': the dead bird dangles from the top of a tall pole stuck in the sward beside a booth. I lost him in the crowd then. But later on in autumn, while rambling round the Chace, there came on a 'skit' of rain, and I made for one of his barns for shelter. There was Hilary in the barn with his men, as busy as they could well be, winnowing oats. It seemed to me that especial care was being taken, and on asking questions, to which the men silently replied with a grin, Hilary presently blurted out that the dust had to be carefully removed, because the grain was for the racing-stable. The dainty creatures up there must have food free from dust, which makes them too thirsty. The hay supplied, for the same reason, had to be shaken before being used. No oats would do under 40 lb. the bushel, and the heavier the better.

Luckett was a man whom every one knew to be 'square'; but, if the talk of the country-side is to be believed, the farmers who have much to do with the stables do not always come off successful. They sometimes become too sharp, and fancy themselves cleverer than a class of men who, if their stature be not great, are probably the keenest of wit. The farmer who obliges them is invariably repaid with lucrative 'tips'; but if he betrays those 'tips' may possibly find his information in turn untrustworthy, and have to sell by auction, and depart to Texas. Luckett avoids such pitfalls by the simple policy of 'squareness', which is, perhaps, the wisest of all. When the 'skit' blew past he took his gun from the corner and stepped over the hatch, and came down the path with me, grumbling that all the grain, even where the crop looked well, had threshed out so light.

Farming had gone utterly to the dogs of late seasons; he thought he should give up the land he rented, and live on the ninety acres freehold. In short, to hear him talk, you would think that he was conferring a very great favour upon his landlord in consenting to hold that six or seven hundred acres at a rent which has not been altered these fifty years at least. But the owner was a very good fellow, and as Hilary said, 'There it is, you see.' My private opinion is that, despite the late bad seasons, Hilary has long been doing remarkably well; and as for his landlord, that he would stand by him shoulder to shoulder if defence were needed.

Much as I admired the timber about the Chace, I could not help sometimes wishing to have a chop at it. The pleasure of felling trees is never lost. In youth, in manhood – so long as the arm can wield the axe – the enjoyment is equally keen. As the heavy tool passes over the shoulder the impetus of the swinging motion lightens the weight, and something like a thrill passes through the sinews. Why is it so pleasant to strike? What secret instinct is it that makes the delivery of a blow with axe or hammer so exhilarating? The wilder frenzy of the sword – the fury of striking with the keen blade, which overtakes men even now when they come hand to hand, and which was once the life of battle – seems to arise from the same feeling. Then, as the sharp edge of the axe cuts deep through the bark into the wood, there is a second moment of gratification. The next blow sends a chip spinning aside; and by-the-bye never stand at the side of a woodman, for a chip may score your cheek like a slash with a knife. But the shortness of man's days will not allow him to cut down many trees. In imagination I sometimes seem to hear the sounds of the axes that have been ringing in the forests of America for a hundred years, and envy the joy of the lumbermen as the tall pines toppled to the fall. Of our English trees there is none so pleasant to chop as the lime; the steel enters into it so easily.

In the enclosed portion of the park at Okebourne the boughs of the trees descended and swept the sward. Nothing but sheep being permitted to graze there, the trees grew in their natural form, the lower limbs drooping downwards to the ground. Hedgerow timber is usually 'stripped' up at intervals, and the bushes, too, interfere with the expansion of the branches; while the boughs of trees standing in the open fields are nibbled off by cattle. But in that part of the park no cattle had fed in the memory of man; so that the lower limbs, drooping by their own weight, came arching to the turf. Each tree thus made a perfect bower.

The old woodmen who worked in the Chace told me it used to be said that elm ought only to be thrown on two days of the year – *i.e.* the 31st of December and the 1st of January. The meaning was that it should be cut in the very 'dead of the year', when the sap had retired, so that the timber might last longer. The old folk took the greatest trouble to get their timber well seasoned, which is the reason why the woodwork in old houses has endured so well. Passing under some elms one June evening, I heard a humming overhead, and found it was caused by a number of bees and humble-bees busy in the upper branches at a great height from the ground. They were probably after the honey-dew. Buttercups do not flourish under trees; in early summer, where elms or oaks stand in the mowing-grass, there is often a circle around almost bare of them and merely green, while the rest of the meadow glistens with the burnished gold of that beautiful flower.

The oak is properly regarded as a slow-growing tree, but under certain circumstances a sapling will shoot up quickly to a wonderful height. When the woodmen cut down a fir plantation in the Chace there was a young oak among it that overtopped the firs, and yet its diameter was so small that it looked no larger than a pole; and the supporting boughs of the firs being now removed it could not uphold itself, but bent so much from the perpendicular as to appear incapable of withstanding a gale. The bark of the oak, when stripped and stacked, requires fine weather to dry it, much the same as hay, so that a wet season like 1879 is very unfavourable.

In the open glades of the Chace there were noble clumps of beeches, and if you walked quietly under them in the still October days you might hear a slight but clear and distinct sound above you. This was caused by the teeth of a squirrel nibbling the beech-nuts, and every now and then down came pieces of husk rustling through the coloured leaves. Sometimes a nut would fall which he had dropped; and yet, with the nibbling sound to guide the eye, it was not always easy to distinguish the little creature. But his tail presently betrayed him among the foliage, far out on a bough where the nuts grew. The husks, if undisturbed, remain on all the winter and till the tree is in full green leaf again; the young nuts are formed about midsummer.

The black poplars are so much like the aspen as to be easily mistaken, especially as their leaves rustle in the same way. But the true aspen has a smooth bark, while that of the black poplar is scored or rough. Woodmen always call the aspen the 'asp', dropping the termination. In the spring the young foliage of the black poplar has a yellow tint. When they cut down the alder poles by the water and peeled them, the sap under the bark as it dried turned as red as if stained. The paths in spring were strewn with the sheaths of the young leaves and buds pushing forth; showers of such brown sheaths came off the hawthorn with every breeze. These, with the catkins, form the first fall from tree and bush. The second is the flower, as the May, and the horse-chestnut bloom, whose petals cover the ground. The third fall is that of the leaf, and the fourth the fruit.

On the Scotch fir the young green cones are formed about the beginning of June, and then the catkin adjacent to the cone is completely covered with quantities of pale yellow farina. If handled, it covers the fingers as though they had been dipped in sulphur-flour; shake the branch and it flies off, a little cloud of powdery particles. The scaly bark takes a ruddy tinge, when the sunshine falls upon it, and would then, I think, be worthy the attention of an artist as much as the birch bark, whose peculiar mingling of silvery white, orange, and brown, painters so often endeavour to represent on canvas. There is something in the Scotch fir, crowned at the top like a palm with its dark foliage, which, in a way I cannot express or indeed analyse, suggests to my mind the far-away old world of the geologists.

In the boughs of the birch a mass of twigs sometimes grows so close and entangled together as to appear like a large nest from a distance when the leaves are off. Even as early as December the tomtits attack the buds, then in their sheaths, of the birch, clinging to the very extremities of the slender boughs. I once found a young birch growing on the ledge of a brick bridge, outside the parapet, and some forty or fifty feet from the ground. It was about four feet high, quite a sapling, and apparently flourishing, though where the roots could find soil it was difficult to discover.

The ash tree is slowly disappearing from many places, and owners of hedgerow and copse would do well to plant ash, which affords a most useful wood. Ash poles are plentiful, but ash timber gets scarcer year by year; for as the present trees are felled there are no young ones rising up to take their place. Consequently ash is becoming dearer, as the fishermen find; for many of the pleasure yachts which they let out in summer are planked with ash, which answers well for boats which are often high and dry on the beach, though it would not do if always in the water. These beach-boats have an oak frame, oak stem and stern-post, beech keel, and are planked with ash. When they require repairing, the owners find ash planking scarce and dear.

Trees may be said to change their garments thrice in the season. In the spring the woods at Okebourne were of the tenderest green, which, as the summer drew on, lost its delicacy of hue. Then came the second or 'midsummer shoot', brightening them with fresh leaves and fresh green. The second shoot of the oak is reddish: there was one oak in the Chace which after midsummer thus became ruddy from the highest to the lowest branch; others did not show the change nearly so much. Lastly came the brown and yellow autumn tints.

Chapter II.

Cicely.　The Brook.

In the kitchen at Lucketts' Place there was a stool made by sawing off about six inches of the butt of a small ash tree. The bark remained on, and it was not smoothed or trimmed in any way. This mere log was Cicely Luckett's favourite seat as a girl; she was Hilary's only daughter. The kitchen had perhaps originally been the house, the rest having been added to it in the course of years as the mode of life changed and increasing civilisation demanded more convenience and comfort. The walls were quite four feet thick, and the one small lattice-window in its deep recess scarcely let in sufficient light, even on a summer's day, to dispel the gloom, except at one particular time.

The little panes, yellow and green, were but just above the ground, looking out upon the road into the rickyard, so that the birds which came searching along among the grasses and pieces of wood thrown carelessly aside against the wall could see into the room. Robins, of course, came every morning, perching on the sill and peering in with the head held on one side. Blackbird and thrush came, but always passed the window itself quickly, though they stayed without fear within a few inches of it on either hand.

There was an old oak table in the centre of the room – a table so solid that young Aaron, the strong labourer, could only move it with difficulty. There was no ceiling properly speaking, the boards of the floor above and a thick beam which upheld it being only whitewashed; and much of that had scaled off. An oaken door led down a few steps into the cellar, and over both cellar and kitchen there sloped a long roof, thatched, whose eaves were but just above the ground.

Now, when there was no one in the kitchen, as in the afternoon, when even the indoor servants had gone out to help in the hayfield, little Cicely used to come in here and sit dreaming on the ash log by the hearth. The rude stool was always placed inside the fireplace, which was very broad for burning wood, faggots and split pieces of timber. Bending over the grey ashes, she could see right up the great broad tunnel of the chimney to the blue sky above, which seemed the more deeply azure, as it does from the bottom of a well. In the evenings when she looked up she sometimes saw a star shining above. In the early mornings of the spring, as she came rushing down to breakfast, the tiny yellow panes of the window which faced the east were all lit up and rosy with the rays of the rising sun.

The beautiful light came through the elms of the rickyard, away from the ridge of the distant Down, and then for the first hour of the day the room was aglow. For quite two hundred years every visible sunrise had shone in at that window more or less, as the season changed and the sun rose to the north of east. Perhaps it was that sense of ancient homeliness that caused Cicely, without knowing why, to steal in there alone to dream, for nowhere else indoors could she have been so far away from the world of to-day.

Left much to herself, she roamed along the hedgerow as now and then a mild day came, soon after the birds had paired, and saw the arrow-shaped, pointed leaves with black spots rising and unrolling at the sides of the ditches. Many of these seemed to die away presently without producing anything, but from some there pushed up a sharply conical sheath, from which emerged the spadix of the arum with its frill. Thrusting a stick into the loose earth of the bank, she found the root, covered with a thick wrinkled skin which peeled easily and left a white substance like a small potato. Some of the old women who came into the kitchen used to talk about 'yarbs', and she was told that this was poisonous and ought not to be touched – the very reason why she slipped into the dry ditch and dug it up. But she started with a sense of guilt as she heard the slow rustle of a snake gliding along the mound over the dead, dry leaves of last year.

In August, when the reapers began to call and ask for work, she found the arum stalks, left alone without leaves, surrounded with berries, some green, some ripening red. As the berries ripen, the stalk grows weak and frequently falls prone of its own weight among the grasses. This noisome fruit of clustering berries, like an ear of maize stained red, they told her was 'snake's victuals', and to be avoided; for, bright as was its colour, it was only fit for reptile's food.

She knew, too, where to find the first 'crazy Betties', whose large yellow flowers do not wait for the sun, but shine when the March wind scatters king's ransoms over the fields. These are the marsh marigolds: there were two places where she gathered them, one beside the streamlet flowing through the 'Mash', a meadow which was almost a water-meadow; and the other inside a withy-bed. She pulled the 'cat's-tails', as she learned to call the horse-tails, to see the stem part at the joints; and when the mowing-grass began to grow long, picked the cuckoo-flowers and nibbled the stalk and leaflets to essay the cress-like taste. In the garden, which was full of old-fashioned shrubs and herbs, she watched the bees busy at the sweet-scented 'honey-plant', and sometimes peered under the sage-bush to look at the 'effets' that hid there.

By the footpath through the meadows there were now small places where the mowers had tried their new scythes as they came home, a little warm with ale perhaps, from the market town. They cut a yard or two of grass as they went through the fields, just to get the swing of the scythe and as a hint to the farmer that it was time to begin. With the first June rose in the hedge the haymaking commenced – the two usually coincide – and then Cicely fluctuated between the haymakers and the mowers, now watching one and now the other. One of the haymaking girls was very proud because she had not lost a single wooden tooth out of her rake, for it is easy to break or pull them out. In the next field the mowers, one behind the other in echelon, left each his swathe as he went. The tall bennets with their purplish anthers, the sorrel, and the great white 'moon-daisies' fell before them. Cicely would watch till perhaps the sharp scythe cut a frog, and the poor creature squealed with the pain.

Then away along the hedge to the pond in the corner, all green with 'creed', or duckweed, when one of the boys about the place would come timidly up to offer a nest of eggs just taken, and if she would speak to him would tell her about his exploits 'a-nisting', about the bombarrel tit – a corruption apparently of nonpareil – and how he had put the yellow juice of the celandine on his 'wurrut' to cure it. Then they pulled the plantain leaves, those that grew by the path, to see which could draw out the longest 'cat-gut'; the sinews, as it were, of the plant stretching out like the strings of a fiddle.

In the next meadow the cows had just been turned into fresh grass, and were lazily rioting in it. They fed in the sunshine with the golden buttercups up above their knees, literally wading in gold, their horns as they held their heads low just visible among the flowers. Some that were standing in the furrows were hidden up to their middles by the buttercups. Their sleek roan and white hides contrasted with the green grass and the sheen of the flowers: one stood still, chewing the cud, her square face expressive of intense content, her beautiful eye – there is no animal with a more beautiful eye than the cow – following Cicely's motions. At this time of the year, as they grazed far from the pens, the herd were milked in the corner of the field, instead of driving them to the yard.

One afternoon Cicely came quietly through a gap in the hedge by this particular corner, thinking to laugh at Aaron's voice, for he milked there and sang to the cows, when she saw him sitting on the three-legged milking-stool, stooping in the attitude of milking, with the bucket between his knees, but firm asleep, and quite alone in his glory. He had had too much ale, and dropped asleep while milking the last cow, and the herd had left him and marched away in stately single file down to the pond, as they always drink after milking. Cicely stole away and said nothing; but presently Aaron was missed and a search made, and he was discovered by the other men still sleeping. Poor 'young Aaron' got into nearly as much disgrace through the brown jug as a poaching uncle of his through his ferrets and wires.

When the moon rose full and lit up the Overboro' road as bright as day, and the children came out from the cottages to their play, Cicely, though she did not join, used to watch their romping dances and picked up the old rhymes they chanted. When the full moon shone in at her bedroom window, Cicely was very careful to turn away or cover her face; for she had heard one of the mowers declare that after sleeping on the hay in the moonlight one night he woke up in the morning almost blind. Besides the meadows around Lucketts' Place, she sometimes wandered further to the edge of Hilary's great open arable fields, where the green corn, before it came out in ear, seemed to flutter, flutter like innumerable tiny flags, as the wind rushed over it.

She learned to rub the ripe ears in her hands to work the grain out of the husk, and then to winnow away the chaff by letting the corn slowly drop in a stream from one palm to the other, blowing gently with her mouth the while. The grain remained on account of its weight, the chaff floating away, and the wheat, still soft though fully formed, could thus be pleasantly tasted. The plaintive notes of the yellowhammer fell from the scanty trees of the wheat-field hedge, and the ploughboy who was put there to frighten away the rooks told her the bird said, repeating the song over and over again, 'A little bit of bread and *no* cheese.' And indeed these syllables, with a lengthening emphasis on the 'no', come ludicrously near to represent the notes. The ploughboy understood them very well, for to have only a hunch of bread and little or no cheese was often his own case.

Two meadows distant from the lower woods of the Chace there is what seems from afar a remarkably wide hedge irregularly bordered with furze. But on entering a gateway in it you find a bridge over a brook, which for some distance flows with a hedge on either side. The low parapet of the bridge affords a seat – one of Cicely's favourite haunts – whence in spring it is pleasant to look up the brook; for the banks sloping down from the bushes to the water are yellow with primroses, and hung over with willow boughs. As the brook is straight, the eye can see under these a long way up; and presently a kingfisher, bright with azure and ruddy hues, comes down the brook, flying but just above the surface on which his reflection travels too. He perches for a moment on a branch close to the bridge, but the next sees that he is not alone, and instantly retreats with a shrill cry.

A moorhen ventures forth from under the arches, her favourite hiding-place, and feeds among the weeds by the shore, but at the least movement rushes back to shelter. A wood-pigeon comes over, flying slowly; he was going to alight on the ash tree yonder, but suddenly espying some one under the cover of the boughs increases his pace and rises higher. Two bright bold bullfinches pass; they have a nest somewhere in the thick hawthorn. A jay, crossing from the fir plantations, stays awhile in the hedge, and utters his loud harsh scream like the tearing of linen. For a few hours the winds are still and the sunshine broods warm over the mead. It is a delicious snatch of spring.

Every now and then a rabbit emerges from the burrows which are scattered thickly along the banks, and, passing among the primroses, goes through the hedge into the border of furze, and thence into the meadow-grass. Some way down the brook they are so numerous as to have destroyed the vegetation on the banks, excepting a few ferns, by their constant movements and scratching of the sand; so that there is a small warren on either side of the water. It is said that they occasionally swim across the broad brook, which is much too wide to jump; but I have never seen such a thing but once. A rabbit already stung with shot and with a spaniel at his heels did once leap at the brook here, and, falling short, swam the remainder without apparent trouble, and escaped into a hole on the opposite shore with his wet fur laid close to the body. But they usually cross at the bridge, where the ground bears the marks of their incessant nightly travels to and fro.

Passing now in the other direction, up the stream from the bridge, the hedges after a while cease, and the brook winds through the open fields. Here there is a pond, to which at night the heron resorts; for he does not care to trust himself between the high hedgerows. In the still shallow, but beyond reach, there floats on the surface a small patch of green vegetation formed of the treble leaves of the water crow-foot. Towards June it will be a brilliant white spot. The slender stems uphold the cup-like flowers two or three inches above the surface, the petals of the purest white with a golden centre. They are the silver buttercups of the brook. Where the current flows slowly the long and somewhat spear-shaped leaves of the water-plantain stand up, and in the summer will be surmounted by a tall stalk with three small pale pink petals on its branches. The leaf can be written on with a pencil, the point tracing letters by removing the green colouring where it passes.

Far larger are the leaves of the water-docks; they sometimes attain to immense size. By the bank the 'wild willow', or water-betony, with its woody stem, willow-shaped leaves, and pale red flowers, grows thickly. Across where there is a mud-bank the stout stems of the willow herb are already tall. They quite cover the shoal, and line the brook like shrubs. They are the strongest and most prominent of all the brook plants. At the end of March or beginning of April the stalks appear a few inches high, and they gradually increase in size, until in July they reach above the waist, and form a thicket by the shore. Not till July does the flower open, so that, though they make so much show of foliage, it is months before any colour brightens it. The red flower comes at the end of a pod, and has a tiny white cross within it; it is welcome, because by August so many of the earlier flowers are fading. The country folk call it the sod-apple, and say the leaves crushed in the fingers have something of the scent of apple-pie.

Farther up the stream, where a hawthorn bush shelters it, stands a knotted fig-wort with a square stem and many branches, each with small velvety flowers. If handled, the leaves emit a strong odour, like the leaves of the elder-bush; it is a coarse-growing plant, and occasionally reaches to a height of between four and five feet, with a stem more than half an inch square. Some ditches are full of it. By the rushes the long purple spike of the loose-strife rises, and on the mudbanks among the willows there grows a tall plant with bunches of flower, the petals a bright yellow: this is the yellow loose-strife. Near it is a herb with a much-divided leaf, and curious flowers like small yellow buttons. Rub one of these gently, and it will give forth a most peculiar perfume – aromatic, and not to be compared with anything else; the tansy once scented will always be recognised.

The large rough leaves of the wild comfrey grow in bunches here and there; the leaves are attached to the stem for part of their length, and the stem is curiously flanged. The bells are often greenish, sometimes white, occasionally faintly lilac; they are partly hidden under the dark-green leaves. Where undisturbed the comfrey grows to a great size, the stems becoming very thick. Green flags hide and almost choke the shallow mouth of a streamlet that joins the brook coming from the woods. Though green above, the flag where it enters its sheath is white.

Tracing it upwards, the brook becomes narrower and the stream less, though running more swiftly; and here there is a marshy spot with willows, and between them some bulrushes and great bunches of bullpolls. This coarse grass forms tufts or cushions, on which snakes often coil in the sunshine. Yet though so rough, in June the bullpoll sends up tall slender stalks with graceful feathery heads, reed-like, surrounded with long ribbons of grass. In the ditches hereabout, and beside the brook itself, the meadow-sweet scents the air; the country-folk call it 'meadow-soot'. And in those ditches are numerous coarse stems and leaves which, if crushed in the fingers, yield a strong parsnip-like smell. The water-parsnip, which is poisonous, is said to be sometimes gathered for watercress; but the palate must be dull, one would think, to eat it, and the smell is a sure test. The blue flower of the brooklime is not seen here; you must look for it where the springs break forth, where its foliage sometimes quite conceals the tiny rill.

These flowers do not, of course, all appear together; but they may be all found in the summer season along the brook, and you should begin to look for them when the brown scum, that sign of coming warmth, rises from the bottom of the waters. Returning to the pond, it may be noticed that the cart-horses when they walk in of a summer's day paw the stream, as if they enjoyed the cool sound of the splash; but the cows stand quite still with the water up to their knees.

There is a spot by a yet more quiet bridge, where the little water-shrews play to and fro where the bank overhangs. As they dive and move under water the reddish-brown back looks of a lighter colour; when they touch the ground they thrust their tiny nostrils up just above the surface. There are many holes of water-rats, but no one would imagine how numerous these latter creatures are. One of Hilary's sons, Hugh, kept some ferrets, and in the summer was put to it to find them enough food. The bird-keepers brought in a bird occasionally, and there were cruel rumours of a cat having disappeared. Still there was not sufficient till he hit on the idea of trapping the water-rats; and this is how he did it.

He took three small twigs and ran them into the bank of the brook at the mouth of the water-rat's hole and just beneath the surface of the stream. These made a platform upon which the gin was placed – the pan, and indeed all the trap, just under the water, which prevented any scent. Whether the rat came out of his hole and plunged to dive or started to swim, or whether he came swimming noiselessly round the bend and was about to enter the burrow, it made no difference; he was certain to pass over and throw the gin. The instant the teeth struck him he gave a jump which lifted the trap off the twig platform, and it immediately sank in the deep water and soon drowned him; for the water-rat, though continually diving, can only stay a short time under water. It proved a fatal contrivance, chiefly, as was supposed, because the gin, being just under the water, could not be smelt. No fewer than eleven rats were thus captured in succession at the mouth of one hole. Altogether 150 were taken in the course of that summer.

Hugh kept a record of them by drawing a stroke with chalk for every rat on the red brick wall of the stable, near his ferret-hutch. He only used a few traps – one was set not at a hole but at a sharp curve of the brook – and the whole of these rats were taken in a part of the brook about 250 to 300 yards in length, just where it ran through a single field. The great majority were water-rats, but there were fifteen or twenty house-rats among them: these were very thin though large, and seemed to be caught as they were migrating; for sometimes several were trapped the same day, and then none (of this kind) for a week or more. Three moorhens were also caught; a fourth was only held by its claw in the gin; this one, not being in the least injured, he let go again.

It had been observed previously that the water-rats, either in making their burrows or for food, gnawed off the young withy-stoles underneath the ground in the withy-beds, and thus killed a considerable amount of withy; but after all this slaughter the withy-beds recovered and bore the finest crop they ever grew. But who could have imagined in walking by the brook that only in its course through a single meadow it harboured 150 rats? Probably, though, some of them came up or down the stream. The ferrets fared sumptuously all the summer.

Chapter III.

A Pack of Stoats.   Birds.

The sweet scent from a beanfield beside the road caused me to linger one summer morning in a gateway under the elms. A gentle south wind came over the beans, bearing with it the odour of their black-and-white bloom. The Overboro' road ran through part of the Okebourne property (which was far too extensive to be enclosed in a ring fence), and the timber had therefore been allowed to grow so that there was an irregular avenue of trees for some distance. I faced the beanfield, which was on the opposite side, leaning back against the gate which led into some of Hilary's wheat. The silence of the highway, the soft wind, the alternate sunshine and shade as the light clouds passed over, induced a dreamy feeling; and I cannot say how long I had been there when something seemed as it were to cross the corners of my half-closed eyes.

Looking up I saw three stoats gallop across the road, not more than ten yards away. They issued from under the footpath, which was raised and had a drain through it to relieve the road of flood-water in storm. The drain was faced with a flat stone, with a small round hole cut in it. Coming from the wheat at my back, the stoats went down into the ditch; thence entered the short tunnel under the footpath, and out at its stone portal, over the road to the broad sward on the opposite side; then along a furrow in the turf to the other hedge, and so into the beanfield. They galloped like racehorses straining for the victory; the first leading, the second but a neck behind, and the third not half a length. The smooth road rising slightly in the centre showed them well; and thus, with the neck stretched out in front and the tail extended in the rear, the stoat appears much longer than on a mound or in the grass.

A second or so afterwards two more started from the same spot; but I was perhaps in the act to move, for before they had gone three yards they saw me and rushed back to the drain. After a few minutes the larger of these two, probably the male, ventured forth again and reached the middle of the road, when he discovered that his more timorous companion had not followed but was only just peeping out. He stopped and elevated his neck some five or six inches, planting the fore-feet so as to lift him up high to see round, while his hindquarters were flush with the road, quite flat in the dust in which his tail was trailing. His reddish body and white neck, the clear-cut head, the sharp ears, and dark eye were perfectly displayed in that erect attitude. As his companion still hesitated he cried twice, as if impatiently, 'check, check' – a sound like placing the tongue against the teeth and drawing it away. But she feared to follow, and he returned to her. Thinking they would attempt to cross again presently, I waited quietly.

A lark came over from the wheat, and, alighting, dusted herself in the road, hardly five yards from the mouth of the drain, and was there some minutes. A robin went still closer – almost opposite the hole; both birds apparently quite unconscious of the bloodthirsty creatures concealed within it. Some time passed, but the two stoats did not come out, and I saw no more of them: they probably retreated to the wheat as I left the gateway, and would remain there till the noise and jar of my footsteps had ceased in the distance. Examining the road, there was a trail where the first three had crossed in quick succession. In the thick white dust their swift feet had left a line drawn roughly yet lightly, the paws leaving not an exact but an elongated, ill-defined impression. But where the fourth stopped, elevated his neck, and cried to his mate, there was a perfect print of the fore-feet side by side. So slight a track would be obliterated by the first cart that came by.

Till that day I had never seen so many as five stoats together hunting in a pack. It would seem as if stoats and weasels had regular routes; for I now recollected that in the previous winter, when the snow was on the ground, I surprised two weasels almost exactly in the same spot. At other times, too, I have seen solitary stoats and weasels (which may have had companions in the hedge) hunting along that mound, both before and since. I was at first going to tell Hilary about the pack, but afterwards refrained, as he would at once proceed to set up gins in the run, while I thought I should like to see the animals again. But I got him to talk about stoats and weasels, and found that he had not himself seen so many together. There was, however, a man about the place who told a tale of some weasels he had seen. It was 'that rascal old Aaron'; but he could not listen to such a fellow. Hilary would tell me nothing further, having evidently a strong dislike to the man.

It seems there were two Aarons – uncle and nephew; old Aaron was the arch-poacher of the parish, young Aaron worked regularly at Lucketts' Place. This young labourer (the man who fell asleep on the milking-stool) was one of the best of his class – a great, powerful fellow, but good-natured, willing, and pleasant to speak to. He was a favourite with many, and with reason, for he had a gentleness of manner beyond his station; and, till you knew his weakness, you could not but take an interest in him. His vice was drink. He was always down at Lucketts' Place; and through him I made acquaintance with his disreputable uncle, who was at first rather shy of me, for he had seen me about with Hilary, and between the two there was a mortal feud. Old Aaron could not keep out of Okebourne Chace, and Hilary was 'down' upon him. Hilary was, indeed, keener than the keepers.

The old poacher saw the weasels in the 'Pitching'. This was a private lane, which ran through the recesses of the Chace where the wood was thickest and most secluded. It had been made for the convenience of communication between the upper and lower farms, and for hauling timber; the gates at each end being kept locked. In one place the lane descended the steepest part of the wooded hill, and in frosty weather it was not easy even to walk down it there. Sarsen stones, gathered out of the way of the plough in the arable fields, had been thrown down in it at various times with the object of making a firm bottom. Rounded and smooth and very hard, these stones, irregularly placed, with gaps and intervals, when slippery with hoar frost were most difficult to walk on. Once or twice men out hunting had been known to gallop down this hill: the extreme of headlong bravado; for if there was any frost it was sure to linger in that shady lane, and a slip of the iron-shod hoof could scarcely fail to result in a broken neck. It was like riding down a long steep flight of steps.

Aaron one day was engaged with his ferret and nets in the Pitching, just at the bottom of the hill, where there grew a quantity of brakefern as tall as the shoulder. It was shrivelled and yellow, but thick enough to give him very good cover. Every now and then he looked out into the lane to see if any one was about, and on one of these occasions saw what he imagined at first to be a colony of rats migrating; but when he came near, racing down the lane, he found they were weasels. He counted fourteen, and thought there were one or two more.

Aaron also told me a curious incident that happened to him very early one morning towards the beginning of spring. The snow was on the ground and the moon was shining brightly as he got on the railway (a few miles from Okebourne) and walked some distance up it: he did not say what for, but probably as the nearest way to a cover. As he entered a deep cutting where the line came round a sharp curve he noticed strange spots upon the snow, and upon examination found it was blood. For the moment he thought there had been an accident; but shortly afterwards he picked up a hare's pad severed from the leg, and next a hare's head, and presently came on a quantity of similar fragments, all fresh. He collected them, and found they had belonged to six hares which had been cut to pieces by a passing train. The animals were so mutilated as not to be of the least use.

When I told Hilary of this, he at once pronounced it impossible, and nothing but one of Aaron's lies. On reflection, however, I am not so sure that it is impossible, nor can I see any reason why the old poacher should invent a falsehood of the kind. It was just a time of the year when hares are beginning to go 'mad', and, as they were not feeding but playing together, they might have strayed up the line just as they do along roads. Most persons must have observed how quietly a train sometimes steals up – so quietly as to be inaudible: a fact that has undoubtedly been the death of many unfortunates. Now, just at this spot there was a sharp curve, and if the driver shut off steam as he ran round it the train very likely came up without a sound. The sides of the cutting being very steep, the hares, when at last they perceived their danger, would naturally rush straight away along the metals. Coming at great speed, the engine would overtake and destroy them: a miserable end for the poor creatures in the midst of their moonlight frolic. But what Aaron laid stress on was the fact that he could not even sell the skins, they were so cut to pieces.

The rooks' nests in the Chace were very numerous, and were

chiefly built in elm trees, but some in tall spruce firs. It was easy to know when the birds had paired, as a couple of rooks could then be often seen perched gravely side by side upon an old nest in the midst of leafless boughs, deliberating about its repair. There were some poplars near a part of the rookery, and when the nests were fully occupied with young the old birds frequently alighted on the very top of an adjacent poplar. The slender brush-like tip of the tree bent with their weight, curving over like a whip, to spring up when they left.

The rooks were fond of maize, boldly descending among the poultry kept in a rickyard within a short distance of their trees. If any one has a clump of trees in which rooks seem inclined to build and it is desired to encourage them, it would appear a good plan to establish a poultry-yard in the same field. They are certain to visit the spot.

One day I watched a rook pursuing a swift and making every effort to overtake and strike it. The rook displayed great power of wing, twisting and turning, now descending or turning on one side to glide more rapidly, and uttering short 'caws' of eagerness or anger; but, just eluding the heavy rush of its pursuer, the swift doubled and darted away before it, as if tempting the enemy to charge, and then enjoying his disappointment. Several other swifts wheeled above at a distance, apparently watching. These evolutions lasted some minutes, rook and swift rising higher and higher into the air until, tired of being chased, the swift went straight away at full speed, easily outstripping the rook, which soon desisted from the attempt to follow.

When birds are thus combating, the chief aim of each is to get above the other, as any elevation gives an advantage. This may be continually noticed in spring, when fighting is always going on, and is as characteristic of the small birds as the larger. At first I thought it was a crow after the swift, but came to the conclusion that it must be a rook because the battle began over the rookery and afterwards the aggressor sailed away to where some rooks were feeding. Nor would a crow have exhibited such agility of wing. Swallows often buffet a crow; but this was a clear case of a rook attacking.

In the country rooks never perch on houses, and but seldom on sheds, unless fresh thatched, when they come to examine the straw, as also on the ricks. But in Brighton, which is a treeless locality, a rook may sometimes be seen on a chimney-pot in the midst of the town, and the pinnacles of the Pavilion are a favourite resort; a whole flock of rooks and jackdaws often wheel about the domes of that building. At the Chace a rook occasionally mounted on a molehill recently thrown up and scattered the earth right and left with his bill – striking now to one side and now to the other. Hilary admitted that rooks destroyed vast quantities of grubs and creeping things, but was equally positive that they feasted on grain; and indeed it could not be denied that a crop of wheat almost ripe is a very favourite resort of a flock. He had seen rooks carry away ears of wheat detached from the stalk to an open spot for better convenience. They would follow the dibbling machine, taking each grain of seed-wheat in succession, guided to the exact spot by the slight depression made by the dibble.

Every evening all the rooks of the neighbourhood gathered into vast flocks and returned to roost in the woods of the Chace. But one winter afternoon there came on the most dense fog that had been known for a length of time, and a flock of rooks on their way as usual to the Chace stopped all night in a clump of trees on the farm a mile from the roosting-place. This the oldest labourer had never known them do before. In the winter just past (1879-80) there were several thick fogs during sharp frost. One afternoon I noticed a small flock of starlings which seemed unable to find their way home to the copse where I knew vast numbers of them roosted. This flock as it grew dusk settled in an elm by the roadside, then removed to another, shaking down the rime from the branches, and a third time wheeled round and perched in an oak. At that hour on ordinary days the starlings would all have been flying fast in a straight line for the copse, but these were evidently in doubt and did not know which direction to take.

Hilary disliked to see the wood-pigeons in his wheat-fields: the wood-pigeon beats the grains out of a wheat-ear with the bill, striking it while on the ground. The sparrows, again, clear the standing wheat-ears, which at a little distance look thin and disarranged, and when handled are empty.

There were many missel-thrushes about the Chace; they are fond of a wooded district. They pack together in summer and part in winter – just opposite in that respect to so many other birds, which separate in warm weather and congregate as it grows cold, so that the lower the temperature the larger the flock. In winter and spring the missel-thrushes fly alone or not more than two together. After their young have left the nest they go in small packs. I saw ten or twelve rise from an arable field on the 18th of June last year; there do not often seem to be more than a dozen together. I have counted ten in a pack on the 16th of September, and seven together as late as the 2nd of October. Soon after that they appear to separate and act on their individual wishes. Starlings in like manner pack after their young can fly, but then they do not separate in autumn.

It may be remarked that by autumn the young missel-thrushes would not only fly well, but would have been educated by the old birds, and would have come to maturity. Their natural independence might then come into play. But these are effects rather than causes, besides which I think birds and animals often act from custom rather than for advantage. Among men customs survive for centuries after the original meaning has been lost. I had always been told by country people that the missel-thrush was a solitary bird, and when I first observed a pack and mentioned it some incredulity was expressed. Very naturally in summer people do not see much but hay and wheat. It was noticed on the farms about the Chace in the springs of 1878 and 1879 that the corncrakes, which had formerly been so numerous and proclaimed their presence so loudly, were scarcely heard at all.

It is a little outside my subject, since it did not occur in the Chace, but the other day a friend was telling me how he had been hunted by bucks while riding a bicycle. He was passing through a forest in the summer, when he suddenly became aware of six or seven bucks coming down a glade after him. The track being rough he could not ride at full speed – probably they would have outstripped him even if he had been able to do so – and they were overtaking him rapidly. As they came up he saw that they meant mischief, and fearing a bad fall he alighted by a tree, behind which he thought to dodge them. But so sooner did he touch the ground than the bucks so furiously rushing after him stopped dead in their career; he stepped towards them, and directly they saw him walking they retreated hastily to a distance.

The first berries to go as the autumn approahces are those of the mountain-ash. Both blackbirds and thrushes began to devour the pale-red bunches hanging on the mountain-ashes as early as the 4th of September last year. Starlings are fond of elder-berries: a flock alighting on a bush black with ripe berries will clear the bunches in a very short time. Haws, or peggles, which often quite cover the hawthorn bushes, are not so general a food as the fruit of the briar. Hips are preferred; at least, the fruit of the briar is the first of the two to disappear. The hip is pecked open (by thrushes. redwings, and blackbirds) at the tip, the seeds extracted, and the part where it is attached to the stalk left, just as if the contents had been sucked out. Greenfinches, too, will eat hips.

Haws are often left even after severe frosts; sometimes they seem to shrivel or blacken, and may not perhaps be palatable then. Missel-thrushes and wood-pigeons eat them. Last winter in the stress of the sharp and continued frosts the greenfinches were driven in December to swallow the shrivelled blackberries still on the brambles. The fruity part of the berries was of course gone, and nothing remained but the seeds or pips, dry and hard as wood; they were reduced to feeding on this wretched food. Perhaps the last of the seeds available are those of the docks.

This is well known to bird-fowlers, and on a dry day in January they take two large bunches of docks – 'red docks' they call them – tied round the centre like faggots and well smeared at the top with birdlime. These are placed on the ground, by a hedge, and near them a decoy goldfinch in a cage. Goldfinches eat dock-seed, and if any approach the decoy-bird calls. The wild bird descends from the hedge to feed on the dock-seed and is caught. Goldfinches go in pairs all the winter and work along the hedges together. In spring the young green buds upon the hawthorn are called 'cuckoo's bread and cheese' by the ploughboys.

Chapter IV.

Hamlet Folk.

It happened one Sunday morning in June that a swarm of bees issued from a hive in a cottage garden near Okebourne church. The queen at first took up her position in an elm tree just outside the churchyard, where a large cluster of bees quickly depended from a bough. Being at a great height the cottager could not take them and, anxious not to lose the swarm, he resorted to the ancient expedient of rattling fire-tongs and shovel together in order to attract them by the clatter. The discordant banging of the fire-irons resounded in the church, the doors being open to admit the summer air; and the noise became so uproarious that the clerk presently, at a sign from the rector, went out to stop it, for the congregation were in a grin. He did stop it, the cottager desisting with much reluctance; but, as if to revenge the bee-master's wrongs, in the course of the day the swarm, quitting the elm, entered the church and occupied a post in the roof.

After a while it was found that the swarm had finally settled there, and were proceeding to build combs and lay in a store of honey. The bees, indeed, became such a terror to nervous people, buzzing without ceremony over their heads as they stood up to sing, and caused such a commotion and buffeting with Prayer-books and fans and handkerchiefs, that ultimately the congregation were compelled to abandon their pews. All efforts to dislodge the bees proving for the time ineffectual, the rector had a temporary reading-desk erected in the porch, and there held the service, the congregation sitting on chairs and forms in the yard, and some on the stone tombs, and even on the sward under the yew tree.

In the warm dry hay-making weather this open-air worship was very pleasant, the flowers in the grass and the roses in the little plots about the tombs giving colour and sweet odours, while the swallows glided gracefully overhead and sometimes a blackbird whistled.

The bees, moreover, interfered with the baptisms, and even caused several marriages to be postponed. Inside the porch was a recess where the women left their pattens in winter, instead of clattering iron-shod down the aisle.

Okebourne village was built in an irregular way on both sides of a steep coombe, just at the verge of the hills, and about a mile from the Chace; indeed, the outlying cottages bordered the park wall. The most melancholy object in the place was the ruins of a windmill; the sails and arms had long disappeared, but the wooden walls, black and rotting, remained. The windmill had its genius, its human representative – a mere wreck, like itself, of olden times. There never was a face so battered by wind and weather as that of old Peter, the owner of the ruin. His eyes were so light a grey as to appear all but colourless. He wore a smock-frock the hue of dirt itself, and his hands were ever in his pockets as he walked through rain and snow beside his cart, hauling flints from the pits upon the Downs.

If the history of the cottage-folk is inquired into it will often be found that they have descended from well-to-do positions in life – not from extravagance or crime, or any remarkable piece of folly, but simply from a long-continued process of muddling away money. When the windmill was new, Peter's forefathers had been, for village people well off. The family had never done anything to bring themselves into disgrace; they had never speculated; but their money had been gradually muddled away, leaving the last little better than a labourer. To see him crawling along the road by his load of flints, stooping forward, hands in pocket, and then to glance at the distant windmill, likewise broken down, the roof open, and the rain and winds rushing through it, was a pitiful spectacle. For that old building represented the loss of hope and contentment in life as much as any once lordly castle whose battlements are now visited only by the jackdaw. The family had, as it were, foundered and gone down.

How they got the stray cattle into the pound it is difficult to imagine; for the gate was very narrow, and neither bullocks nor horses like being driven into a box. The copings of the wall on one side had been pushed over, and lay in a thick growth of nettles: this, almost the last of old village institutions, was, too, going by degrees to destruction.

Every hamlet used to have its representative fighting-man – often more than one – who visited the neighbouring villages on the feast days, when there was a good deal of liquor flowing, to vaunt of their prowess before the local champions. These quickly gathered, and after due interchange of speeches not unlike the heroes of Homer, who harangue each other ere they hurl a spear, engaged in conflict dire. There was a regular feud for many years between the Okebourne men and the Clipstone 'chaps'; and never did the stalwart labourers of those two villages meet without falling to fisticuffs with right goodwill. Nor did they like each other at all the worse, and after the battle drank deeply from the same quart cups. Had these encounters found an historian to put them upon record, they would have read something like the wars (without the bloodshed) between the little Greek cities, whose population scarcely exceeded that of a village, and between which and our old villages there exists a certain similarity. A simplicity of sentiment, an unconsciousness as it were of themselves, strong local attachments and hatreds, these they had in common, and the Okebourne and Clipstone men thwacked and banged each other's broad chests in true antique style.

Hilary said that when he was a boy almost all the cottages in the place had a man or woman living in them who had attained to extreme old age. He reckoned up cottage after cottage to me in which he had known old folk up to and over eighty years of age. Of late the old people seemed to have somehow died out: there were not nearly so many now.

Okebourne Wick, a little hamlet of fifteen or twenty scattered houses, was not more than half a mile from Lucketts' Place; on the Overboro' road, which passed it, was a pleasant roadside inn, where, under the sign of The Sun, very good ale was sold. Most of the farmers dropped in there now and then, not so much for a glass as a gossip, and no one from the neighbouring villages or from Overboro' town ever drove past without stopping. In the 'tap' of an evening you might see the labourers playing at 'chuckboard', which consists in casting a small square piece of lead on to certain marked divisions of a shallow tray-like box placed on the trestle-table. The lead, being heavy, would stay where it fell; the rules I do not know, but the scene reminded me of the tric-trac contests depicted by the old Dutch painters.

Young Aaron was very clever at it. He pottered round the inn of an evening and Saturday afternoons, doing odd jobs in the cellar with the barrels; for your true toping spirit loves to knock the hoops and to work about the cask, and carry the jugs in answer to the cry for some more 'tangle-legs' – for thus they called the strong beer. Sometimes a labourer would toast his cheese on a fork in the flame of the candle. In the old days, before folk got so choice of food and delicate of palate, there really seemed no limit to the strange things they ate. Before the railways were made, herds of cattle had of course to travel the roads, and often came great distances. The drovers were at the same time the hardiest and the roughest of men in that rough and hardy time. As night came on, after seeing their herd safe in a field, they naturally ate their supper at the adjacent inn. Then sometimes, as a dainty treat with which to finish his meal, a drover would call for a biscuit, large and hard, as broad as his hand, and, taking the tallow candle, proceed to drip the grease on it till it was well larded and soaked with the melted fat.

At that date, before the Government stamp had been removed from newspapers, the roadside inn was the centre and focus of all intelligence. When the first railway was constructed up in the North the Okebourne folk, like the rest of the world, were with good reason extremely curious about this wonderful invention, and questioned every passer-by eargerly for information. But no one could describe it, till at last a man, born in the village, but who had been away for some years soldiering, returned to his native place. He had been serving in Canada and came through Liverpool, and thus saw the marvel of the age. At The Sun the folk in the evening crowded round him, and insisted upon knowing what a steam-engine was like. He did his best to describe it, but in vain; they wanted a familiar illustration, and could not be satisfied till the soldier, by a happy inspiration, said the only thing to which he could compare a locomotive was a great cannon on a timber-carriage. To us who are so accustomed to railways it seems a singular idea; but, upon reflection, it was not so inapt, considering the audience had seen or heard something of cannons, and were well acquainted with timber-carriages. The soldier wished to convey the notion of a barrel or boiler mounted on wheels.

They kept up the institution of the parish constable, as separate and distinct from the policeman, till very recently at Okebourne, though it seems to have lapsed long since in many country places. One year Hilary, with much shrugging of shoulders, was forced into the office; and during his term there was a terrible set-to between two tribes of gipsies in the Overboro' road. They fought like tigers, making the lovely summer day hideous with their cries and shrieks – the women fiercer by far, tearing each other's hair. One fiendish creature drew her scissors, and using them like a stiletto, drove the sharp point into a sister 'gip's' head.

'Where's the constable?' was the cry. Messengers rushed to Lucketts' Place; the barn, the sheds, the hayfield, all were searched in vain – Hilary had quite disappeared. At the very first sound he had slipped away to look at some cattle in Chequer's Piece, the very last and outlying field of the farms, full a mile away, and when the messengers got to Chequer's Piece of course he was up on the Down. So much for the parish constable's office – an office the farmers shirked whenever they could, and would not put in force when compelled to accept it.

How could a resident willingly go into a neighbour's cottage and arrest him without malice and scandal being engendered? If he did his duty he was abused; if he did not do it, it was hinted that he favoured the offender. As for the 'gip' who was stabbed, nothing more was heard of it; she 'traipsed' off with the rest.

Sometimes when the 'tangle-legs' got up into their heads the labourers felt an inclination to resume the ancient practices of their forefathers. Then you might see a couple facing each other in the doorway, each with his mug in one hand, and the other clenched, flourishing their knuckles. 'Thee hit I'. 'Thee come out in th' road and I'll let thee knaw'. The one knew very well that the other dared not strike him in the house, and the other felt certain that, however entreated, nothing would induce his opponent to accept the invitation and 'come out into th' road.'

The shadows of the elm have so far to fall that they become enlarged and lose the edge upon reaching the ground. I noticed this one moonlight night in early June while sitting on a stile where the footpath opened on the Overboro' road. Presently I heard voices, and immediately afterwards a group came round the curve of the highway. There were three cottage women, each with a basket and several packages; having doubtless been into Overboro' town shopping, for it was Saturday. They walked together in a row; and in front of them, about five yards ahead, came a burly labourer of the same party, carrying in his arms a large clock.

He had taken too much ale, and staggered as he walked, two steps aside to one forward, and indeed could hardly keep upright. His efforts to save himself and the clock from destruction led to some singular flexures of the body, and his feet traced a maze as he advanced, hugging the clock to his chest. The task was too much for his over-taxed patience: just opposite the stile he stood still, held his load high over his head, and shouting, 'Dang th' clock!' hurled it with all his force thirty feet against the mound, at the same time dropping a-sprawl. The women, without the least excitement or surprise, quietly endeavoured to assist him up; and, as he resisted, one of them remarked in the driest matter-of-fact tone, 'Ourn be just like un – as contrary as the wind.' She alluded to her own husband.

When I mentioned this incident afterwards to Mrs. Luckett, she said the troubles the cottage women underwent on account of the 'beer' were past belief. One woman who did some work at the farmhouse kept her cottage entirely by her own exertions; her husband doing nothing but drink. He took her money from her by force, nor could she hide it anywhere but what he would hunt it out. At last in despair she dropped the silver in the jug on the wash-hand basin, and had the satisfaction of seeing him turn everything topsy-turvy in a vain attempt to find it. As he never washed, it never occurred to him to look in the water-jug.

The cottage women when they went into Overboro' shopping, she said, were the despair of the drapers. A woman, with two or three more to chorus her sentiments, would go into a shop and examine half-a-dozen dress fabrics, rubbing each between her work-hardened fingers and thumb till the shopkeeper winced, expecting to see it torn. After trying several and getting the counter covered she would push them aside, contemptuously remarking, 'I don't like this yer shallygallee (flimsy) stuff. Haven't 'ee got any gingham tackle?' Whereat the poor draper would cast down a fresh roll of stoutest material with the reply: 'Here, ma'am. Here's something that will wear like pin-wire.' This did better, but was declared to be 'gallus dear'.

Even within recent years, now and then a servant-girl upon entering service at the farmhouse would refuse to touch butcher's meat. She had never tasted anything but bacon at home, and could only be persuaded to eat fresh meat with difficulty, being afraid she should not like it. One girl who came from a lonely cottage in a distant 'coombe-bottom' of the Downs was observed never to write home or attempt to communicate with her parents. She said it was of no use; no postman came near, and the letters they wrote or the letters written to them never reached their destination. 'Coombe-bottom' is a curious duplication – either word being used to indicate a narrow valley or hollow. An unfortunate child who lived there had never been so well since the stone roller went over his head. She had a lover, but he was 'a gurt hummocksing noon-naw,' so she was not sorry to leave him. The phrase might be translated, 'great loose-jointed idiot.'

They sometimes had lettuce-pudding for dinner, and thought nothing of eating raw bacon. In the snow the men wound haybands round their legs to serve as gaiters, and found it answered admirably. One poor girl had been subject to fits ever since a stupid fellow, during the haymaking, jokingly picked up a snake and threw it round her neck. Yet even in that far-away coombe-bottom they knew enough to put an oyster-shell in the kettle to prevent incrustation.

The rules of pronunciation understood about Okebourne seemed to consist in lengthening the syllables that are usually spoken quick, and shortening those that are usually long. Hilary said that years ago it really appeared as if there was something deficient in the organs of the throat among the labourers, for there were words they positively could not pronounce. The word 'reservoir', for instance, was always 'tezzievoy'; they could not speak the word correctly. He could not explain to me a very common expression among the men when they wished to describe anything unusual or strange for which they had no exact equivalent. It was always 'a sort of a meejick'. By degrees, however, we traced it back to 'menagerie'. The travelling shows of wild beasts at first so much astonished the villagers that everything odd and curious became a menagerie, afterwards corrupted to 'meejick'.

'Caddle no man's cattle' was a favourite proverb with a population who were never in a hurry. 'Like shot out of a show'l', to express extreme nimbleness, was another. A comfortless, bare apartment was 'gabern'; anything stirred with a pointed instrument was 'ucked' – whether a cow 'ucked' the fogger with her horn or the stable was cleaned out with the fork. The verb 'to uck' was capable indeed of infinite conjugation, and young Aaron, breaking off a bennet, once asked me to kindly 'uck' a grain of hay-dust out of his eye with it. When a heron rose out of the brook 'a moll ern flod away.'

With all their apparent simplicity some of the cottage folk were quite up to the value of appearances. Old Aaron had a little shop; he and his wife sold small packets of tea, tobacco, whipcord, and so forth. Sometimes while his wife was weighing out the sugar, old Aaron – wretched old deceiver – would come in rustling a crumpled piece of paper as if it were a banknote, and handing it to her with much impressiveness of manner whisper loudly, 'Now you take un and put un away; and mind you don't mix um. You put he along with the fives and not with the tens.'

Hilary once showed me the heel of a boot which had just been mended by the hedge carpenter and cobbler who worked for him; and offered to bet that not all the scientific people in Europe, with microscope, spectrum analysis, all their appliances, could tell what leather the new heel-piece was made of. Unable to guess, I gave it up; it was of bacon. A pig that was never a 'good doer' was found in a ditch dead. There is always a competition among the labourers for a dead pig or sheep; it was the cobbler's turn, and he had it, cut it up, and salted it down. But when in course of time he came to partake of his side of bacon, behold it was so tough and dried up that even he could not gnaw it. The side hung in the cottage for months, for he did not like to throw it away, and could not think what to do with it, for the dogs could not eat it. At last the old fellow hit upon the notion of using it as leather to mend shoes; so half his customers walked about the world on bacon heels.

So far as I could discover, the cottage folk did not now use many herbs. They made tea sometimes of the tormentil, whose little yellow flowers appear along the furrows. The leaves of the square-stemmed figwort, which they called 'cresset' or 'cressil', were occasionally placed on a sore; and the yarrow – locally 'yarra' – was yet held in estimation as a salve or ointment.

It would be possible for any one to dwell a long time in the midst of a village, and yet never hear anything of this kind and obtain no idea whatever of the curious mixture of the grotesque, the ignorance and yet cleverness, which go to make up hamlet life. But so many labourers and labouring women were continually in and out of the kitchen at Lucketts' Place that I had an opportunity of gathering these items from Mrs. Luckett and Cicely. Years since they had employed even more labour, before machinery came into use so much: then as many as twenty-four women might have been counted in one hayfield, all in regular rank like soldiers, turning the hay 'wallows' with their rakes. 'There's one thing now you have forgotten,' said Cicely. 'They pick the canker-roses off the briars and carry them in the pocket as a certain preventive of rheumatism.'

Chapter V.

Wind-Anemones.   The Fishpond.

The only spot about the Chace where the wind-anemones grew was in a small detached copse of ash-poles nearly a mile from the great woods. Between the stoles, which were rather far apart, the ground was quite covered in spring with dark-green vegetation, so that it was impossible to walk there without treading down the leaves of bluebells, anemones, and similar woodland plants. But if you wished to see the anemones in their full beauty it was necessary to visit the copse frequently; for if you forgot it, or delayed a fortnight, very likely upon returning you would find that their fleeting loveliness was over. Their slender red stems rise but a few inches, and are surrounded with three leaves; the six white petals of the cup-shaped flower droop a little and have a golden centre. Under the petal is a tinge of purple, which is sometimes faintly visible through it. The leaves are not only three in number, but are each cut deeply thrice; they are hardy, but the flower extremely delicate.

On the banks dividing the copse from the meadows around it the blue dog-violets, which have no perfume, often opened so large and wide as to resemble pansies. They do not appear like this till just as their flowering time is almost over. The meadows by the copse were small, not more than two or three acres each. One which was marshy was white for weeks together with the lady's-smock or cuckoo-flower. The petals of these flowers are silvery white in some places, in others tinted with lilac. The hues of wild flowers vary with their situation: in shady woodlands the toadflax or butter-and-eggs is often pale – a sulphur colour; upon the Downs it is a deep and beautiful yellow. In a ditch of this marshy meadow was a great bunch of woodruff, above whose green whorls the white flowers were lifted. Over them the brambles arched, their leaves growing in fives, and each leaf prickly. The bramble-shoots, as they touch the ground, take root and rise again, and thus would soon cross a field were they not cut down.

Pheasants were fond of visiting this copse, following the hedge-rows to it from the Chace, and they always had one or more nests in it. A green woodpecker took it in his route, though he did not stay long, there not being many trees. These birds seem to have their regular rounds; there are some copses where they are scarcely ever heard. They prefer old trees; where there is much large and decaying timber, there the woodpeckers come. Such little meadows as these about the copse are the favourite resort of birds and the very home of flowers – more so than extensive woods like the Chace, or the open pastures and arable fields. Thick hedgerows attract birds, and behind such cover their motions may be watched. There is, too, more variety of bush and tree.

In one such hedgerow leading from the copse the maple-bushes in spring were hung with the green flowers which, though they depend in their season from so many trees, as the oak, are perhaps rarely observed. The elder-bushes in full white bloom scented the air for yards around both by night and day; the white bloom shows on the darkest evening. Besides several crab-stoles – the buds of the crab might be mistaken for thorns growing pointed at the extreme end of the twigs – there was a large crab tree, which bore a plentiful crop. The lads sharpen their knives by drawing the blade slowly to and fro through a crab-apple; the acid of the fruit eats the steel like aquafortis. They hide stores of these crabs in holes in the hayricks, supposing them to improve by keeping. There, too, they conceal quantities of the apples from the old orchards, for the fruit in them is often almost as hard and not much superior in flavour to the crab. These apples certainly become more mellow after several months in the warm hay.

A wild 'plum', or bullace, grew in one place; the plum about twice the size of a sloe, with a bloom upon the skin like the cultivated fruit, but lacking its sweetness. Yet there was a distinct difference of taste: the 'plum' had not got the extreme harshness of the sloe. A quantity of dogwood occupied a corner; in summer it bore a pleasing flower; in the autumn, after the black berries appeared upon it, the leaves became a rich bronze colour, and some when the first frosts touched them curled up at the edge and turned crimson. There were two or three guelder-rose bushes – the wild shrub – which were covered in

June with white bloom; not in snowy balls like the garden variety, but flat and circular, the florets at the edge of the circle often whitest, and those in the centre greenish. In autumn the slender boughs were weighed down with heavy bunches of large purplish berries, so full of red juice as to appear on the point of bursting. As these soon disappeared they were doubtless eaten by birds.

Besides the hawthorn and briar there were several species of willow – the snake-skin willow, so called because it sheds its bark; the 'snap-willow', which is so brittle that every gale breaks off its feeble twigs, and pollards. One of these, hollow and old, had upon its top a crowd of parasites. A bramble had taken root there, and hung over the side; a small currant-bush grew freely – both, no doubt, unwittingly planted by birds – and finally the bines of the noxious bitter-sweet or nightshade, starting from the decayed wood, supported themselves among the willow-branches, and in autumn were bright with red berries. Ash-stoles, the buds on whose boughs in spring are hidden under black sheaths; nut-tree stoles, with ever-welcome nuts – always stolen here, but on the Downs, where they are plentiful, staying till they fall; young oak growing up from the butt of a felled tree. On these oak-twigs sometimes, besides the ordinary round galls, there may be found another gall, larger, and formed, as it were, of green scales one above the other.

Where shall we find in the artificial and, to my thinking, tasteless pleasure-grounds of modern houses so beautiful a shrubbery as this old hedgerow? Nor were evergreens wanting, for the ivy grew thickly, and there was one holly-bush – not more, for the soil was not affected by holly. The tall cow-parsnip or 'gicks' rose up through the bushes; the great hollow stem of the angelica grew at the edge of the field, on the verge of the grass, but still sheltered by the brambles. Some reeds early in spring thrust up their slender green tubes, tipped with two spear-like leaves. The reed varies in height according to the position in which it grows. If the hedge has been cut it does not reach higher than four or five feet; when it springs from a deep, hollow corner, or with bushes to draw it up, you can hardly touch its tip with your walking-stick. The leaders of the black bryony, lifting themselves above the bushes, and having just there nothing to cling to, twist around each other, and two bines thus find mutual support where one alone would fall of its own weight.

In the watery places the sedges send up their dark flowers, dusted with light yellow pollen, rising above the triangular stem with its narrow, ribbed leaf. The reed-sparrow or bunting sits upon the spray over the ditch with its carex grass and rushes; he is a graceful bird, with a crown of glossy black. Hops climb the ash and hang their clusters, which impart an aromatic scent to the hand that plucks them; broad burdock leaves, which the mouchers put on the tops of their baskets to shield their freshly gathered watercresses from the sunshine; creeping avens, with buttercup-like flowers and long stems that straggle across the ditch, and in autumn are tipped with a small ball of soft spines; mints, strong-scented and unmistakable; yarrow, white and sometimes a little lilac, whose flower is perhaps almost the last that the bee visits. In the middle of October I have seen a wild bee on a last stray yarrow.

On the higher and drier bank some few slender square stems of betony, with leaves in pairs like wings, stand up tall and stiff as the summer advances. The labiate purplish flowers are all at the top; each flower is set in the cup by a curve at the lesser end, like a crook; the leaves and stalk are slightly rough, and have an aromatic bitter perfume when crushed. On the flower of a great thistle a moth has alighted, and hidden under its broad wing is a humble-bee, the two happy together and neither interfering with the other. Sometimes a bee will visit the white rose on the briar.

Near the gateway, on the edge of the trodden ground, grows a tall, stout, bushy plant, like a shrub, with pale greyish-green leaves, much lobed and divided: the top of each branch in August is thick with small whitish-green flowers tipped with brown. These, if rubbed in the hand, emit a stong and peculiar scent, with a faint flavour of lavender, and yet quite different. This is the mugwort. Still later on, under the shade of the trees on the mound, there appear bunches of a pale herb, with greenish labiate flowers, and a scent like hops: it is the woodsage, and if tasted the leaf will be found extremely bitter.

In the mornings of autumn the webs of the spiders hang along the hedge bowed a little with dew, like hammocks of gossamer slung from thorn to thorn. Then the hedge-sparrows, perching on the topmost boughs of the hawthorn, cry 'peep-peep' mournfully; the heavy dew on the grass beneath arranges itself in two rows of drops along the edges of the blades. From the day when the first leaf appears upon the hardy woodbine, in the early year, to the time when the partridge finds the eggs in the ant-hill, and on again till the last harebell dies, there is always something beautiful or interesting in these great hedgerows. Indeed, it is impossible to exhaust them. I have omitted the wild geranium with its tiny red petals scarce seen in the mass of green, the mosses, the ferns, and have scarcely said a word about the living creatures that haunt it. But then one might begin to write a book about a hedgerow when a boy and find it incomplete in old age.

A much-neglected path led from the park through some fir plantations down to the fishpond. After the first turn of the narrow track the close foliage of the firs, through which nothing could be seen, shut out the world with green walls. The strip of blue sky visible above was wider than the path, because the trees sloped away somewhat, their branches shortening towards the top; still it was so contracted that a passing woodpigeon was seen but for a second as he went over. Every step carried me into deeper silence – the sudden call of a jay was startling in its harsh contrast. Presently the path widened where the thickly planted firs were succeeded by sycamores, horse-chestnuts, alders, and aspen – trees which stand farther apart, and beneath which some underwood grew. Here there were thickets of hawthorn and bramble and elder bushes which can find no place among firs.

The ground now sloped rapidly down into a hollow, and upon this descent numbers of skeleton leaves were scattered. There was no other spot all over the Chace where they could be seen like this; you might walk for hours and not find one, yet here there were hundreds. Sometimes they covered the ground in layers, several leaves one on the other. In spring violets pushed up through them and blue-bells – sweet hope rising over grey decay.

Lower down a large pond almost filled the hollow. It was surrounded on three sides by trees and thickets; on the fourth an irregular margin of marshy grass extended. Floating leaves of weeds covered the surface of the water; these weeds had not been disturbed for years, and there was no check to their growth except their own profusion, for they choked each other. The pond had long ceased to supply fish for the table. Before railways brought the sea so near, such ponds were very useful. At that time almost everything consumed came from the estate itself: the bread, the beef, the mutton, the venison, game, fish, all was supplied by the adjacent woods, the fields, or the water. The lord in old days hunted the deer on his own domain, brought down game with a crossbow or captured it with nets, and fished or netted his own streams and ponds. These great parks and chaces enclosed everything, so that it was within easy reach of his own door. Sometimes the lord and his visitors strolled out to see the fishponds netted.

This pond had originally been one of a series, but the others had been drained and added to the meadows. It was said to be staked at the bottom to prevent illicit netting; but if so, the stakes by this time were probably rotten or buried in mud formed from the decaying weeds, the fallen leaves, and branches which were gradually closing it up. A few yards from the edge there was a mass of ivy through which a little brown thatch could be distinguished, and on approaching nearer this low roof was found to cover the entrance to a cave. It was an icehouse excavated in the sloping ground or bank, in which, 'when George the Third was King', the ice of the ponds had been preserved to cool the owner's wine in summer. Ice was then a luxury for the rich only; but when so large a supply arrived from America, a supply increased by freezing machines, the icehouse lost its importance. The door, once so jealously closed, was gone, and the dead leaves of last year had gathered in corners where the winds had whirled them.

The heat of a warm June day seemed still more powerful in this hollow. The sedges, into which two or three moorhens had retired at my approach, were still, and the leaves on the boughs overhanging the water were motionless. Where there was a space free from weeds – a deeper hole near the bank – a jack basked at the surface in the sunshine. High above on the hill stood a tall dead fir, from whose trunk the bark was falling; it had but one branch, which stood out bare and stark across the sky. There came a sound like distant thunder, but there were no clouds overhead, and it was not possible to see far round. Pushing gently through the hawthorn bushes and ash-stoles at the farther end of the pond, I found a pleasant little stream rushing swiftly over a clear chalky bottom, hastening away down to the larger brook.

Beyond it rose a mound and hedgerow, up to which came the meadows, where, from the noise, the cattle seemed racing to and fro, teased by insects. Tiny black flies alighting on my hands and face, irritated the skin; the haymakers call them 'thunder-flies'; but the murmur of the running water was so delicious that I sat down on a bulging tree-root, almost over the stream, and listened to the thrushes singing. Had it been merely warm they would have been silent. They do not sing in dry sunshine, but they knew what was coming; so that there is no note so hated by the haymaker as that of the thrush. The birds were not in the firs, but in the ash-trees along the course of the rill.

The voice of the thrush is the most 'cultivated', so to speak, of all our birds: the trills, the runs, the variations, are so numerous and contrasted. Not even the nightingale can equal it: the nightingale has not nearly such command: the thrush seems to know no limit. I own I love the blackbird best, but in excellence of varied music the thrush surpasses all. Few birds, except those that are formed for swimming, come to a still pond. They like a clear running stream; they visit the sweet running water for drinking and bathing. Dreaming away the time, listening to the rush of the water bubbling about the stones, I did not notice that the sky had become overcast, till suddenly a clap of thunder near at hand awakened me. Some heavy drops of rain fell; I looked up and saw the dead branch of the fir on the hill stretched out like a withered arm across a black cloud.

Hastening back to the icehouse, I had barely entered the doorway when the lightning, visible at noonday, flashed red and threatening, the thunder crackled and snapped overhead, and the rain fell in a white sheet of water. There were but two of these overpowering discharges with their peculiar crack and snap; the electricity passed on quickly, and the next clap roared over the woods. But the rain was heavier than before, the fall increased after every flash, however distant, and the surface of the pond was threshed by the drops which bore down with them many leaves weakened by blight.

Doubtless the mowers in the meadows had hidden the blades of their scythes under the swathe, and the haymakers had placed their prongs in the ditches: nothing is so likely to attract a shock of lighting as a prong carried on the shoulder with the bright steel points upwards. In the farmhouses the old folk would cover up the looking-glasses lest the quicksilver should draw the electric fluid. The haymakers will tell you that sometimes when they have been standing under a hedge out of a storm a flash of lightning has gone by with a distinct sound like 'swish', and immediately afterwards the wet ground has sent forth a vapour, or, as they say, smoked.

Woodpigeons and many other birds seem to come home to woods and copses before and during a storm. The woodpigeon is one of the freest of birds to all appearance: he passes over the highest trees and goes straight away for miles. Yet, though it is usual to speak of wild birds and of their freedom, the more you watch their ways the more you feel that the wildest have their routes and customs: that they do not act entirely from the impulse of the moment, but have their unwritten laws. How do the gnats there playing under the horse-chestnut boughs escape being struck down by the heavy raindrops, each one of which looks as if it would drown so small a creature? The numbers of insects far exceed all that words can express: consider the clouds of midges that often dance over a stream. One day, chancing to glance at a steeple, I saw what looked like thin smoke issuing from the top of it. Now it shot out in a straight line from the gilded beak of the weathercock, now veered about, or declined from the vane. It was an innumerable swarm of insects, whose numbers made them visible at that height.

Some insects are much more powerful than would be supposed. A garden was enclosed with fresh palings formed of split oak so well seasoned (split oak is the hardest of wood) that it was difficult to train any creepers against them, for a nail could not be driven in without the help of a bradawl. Passing along the path one afternoon I heard a peculiar rasping sound like a very small saw at work, and found it proceeded from four wasps biting the oak for the materials of their nest. The noise they made was audible four or five yards away, and upon looking closer I found the palings all scored and marked in short shallow grooves. The scores and marks extended along that part of the palings where the sunshine usually fell; there were none on the shady side, the wasps preferring to work in the sunlight.

Soon the clouds began to break, and then the sun shone on innumerable rain-drops. I at once started forth, knowing that such a storm is often followed by several lesser showers with brief intervals between. The deserted ice-house was rarely visited – only, perhaps, when some borage was wanted to put in summer drinks. For a thick growth of borage had sprung up by it, where perhaps a small garden patch had once been cultivated, for there was a pear-tree near. The plant, with its scent of cucumber, grew very strong; the blue flowers when fallen, if they had not been observed when growing, might be supposed to have been inserted exactly upside down to their real manner of attachment. In autumn the leaves of the pear-tree reddened, and afterwards the ivy over the entrance to the icehouse flowered; then in the cold months of early spring the birds came for the ivy-berries.

Chapter VI.

A Farmer of the Olden Times.

The winding paths traced by a hare in spring as he roams over an arable field show that he must cover a mile within a furlong. From a gateway one morning I watched a hare busy in this way, restlessly passing to and fro over the 'lands'. Every motion was visible, because, although the green wheat was rising in an adjacent field, no crop had yet appeared here. Now the hare came direct towards me, running down a furrow; then he turned short and followed a course like the letter V; next he crossed the angle of the field and came back along the shore of the ditch, under the hedge. Then away to the centre of the field, where he stayed some time exploring up one furrow and down another, his ears and the hump of his back only seen above the clods.

But suddenly he caught a scent of something that alarmed him, and away he went full speed: when on the open ground the peculiar way in which the hind limbs are thrown forward right under the body, thus giving an immense 'stride', was clearly displayed. I had been so interested in the hare that I had not observed Hilary coming along on the other side of the low fence, looking at his wheat. The hare, busy as he was and seeming to see nothing, had crossed his 'wind'. Hilary came to me, and we walked together along the waggon-track, repassing the the wheat. He was full about it: he was always grieving over the decadence of the wheat crop.

There was nothing, he went on, so pleasant to watch as it came up, nothing that required so much care and skill, nothing so thoroughly associated with the traditions of English farming as wheat, and yet nothing so disappointing. Foreign importations had destroyed this very mainstay. Now, that crop which he had just left had 'tillered out' well; but what profit should he get from the many stalks that had tillered or sprung from each single grain, thus promising a fiftyfold return? It had been well got in, and, as the old saw had it, 'Well sown, half grown'; it had been in the ground the proper time ('Long in the bed, big in the head'); but likely enough the price next autumn would not much more than pay the expenses of preparation.

The thunderstormn before Christmas was not perhaps a favourable omen, since

> Winter's thunder and summer's flood
> Bode old England no good.

Last year showed that 'summer's flood' was as destructive as in the old time. But then there would have been a rise of prices, according to the saying, -

> When the vale shall feed the hill,
> Every man shall eat his fill.
> But when the hill shall feed the vale,
> The penny loaf shall be but small.

Now, last season, so far as our home harvests were concerned, the 'hill' did feed the 'vale', but the penny loaves were as large and as plentiful as usual, owing to foreign grain. In those old days, seventy or eighty years since, the whole population of the kingdom watched the weather with anxiety; and it was then that the signs and tokens of birds and plants and the set of the wind at particular times were regarded as veritable oracles to be inquired into not without fear and trembling.

Hilary heard all about it when he was a lad from old Jonathan, who had a corn-farm up on the hills, and where he used to go to plough. Hilary never stated the exact degree, but there was some relationship between them – two branches, I fancy, of the same family. He seemed to have a very bitter memory of the old man (now dead), who had been a hard master to him in his youth; besides which, some family jar had arisen over money matters; still, he was fond of quoting Jonathan in reference to wheat and the heyday of corn-farming. Jonathan remembered when a load of wheat fetched 55*l.* – a load being five quarters or ten sacks – or 11*l* a quarter. The present average of wheat was about 2*l.* 6*s.* per quarter. At the same time bread was at 3*s*. a gallon; it is now about 1*s*.6*d*. The wages of an agricultural labourer were 6*s* a week. It was gambling, positive gambling, in the staff of life.

No farmer was held in any esteem if he did not keep his wheat ricks till harvest came again before threshing them out; men grew rich suddenly and knew not what to do with their money. Farmers who had been brought up 'hard', living like labourers, working like labourers, and with little more amusement than labourers, all at once found their pockets full of coin. The wheat they had been selling at 5*l*. a load ran up to 50*l*. With their purses thus crammed full, what were they to do? There was nothing but drink, and they did drink.

In those days the farmer in his isolated homestead was more cut off from the world than the settler at the present time in the backwoods or on the prairies. The telegraph wires span the continent of America, and are carried across the dry deserts of Australia. Wherever the settler may be, he is never very far from the wires or the railway; the railway meets the ocean steamer; and we can form no conception of the utter lack of communication in the old world of our immediate forefathers. The farmer, being away from the main road and the track of the mail coaches, knew no one but his neighbours, saw no one, and heard but little. Amusements there were none, other than could be had at the alehouse or by riding into the market town to the inn there. So that when this great flush of prosperity came upon them, old Jonathan and his friends had nothing to do but drink.

Up at The Idovers, as his place was called, a lonely homestead on a plain between the Downs, they used to assemble, and at once put up the shutters, whether it was dark or not, not wishing to know whether it was day or night. Sometimes the head carter would venture in for instructions, and be gruffly told to take his team and do so and so. 'Eez, zur,' he would reply, 'uz did thuck job isterday.' His master had ordered him to do it the day before, but was oblivious that twenty-four hours had passed. The middle-aged men stood this continuous drinking without much harm, their constitutions having become hardened and 'set', but it killed off numbers of the younger men.

They drank ale principally – strong ale, for at that time in lonely farmhouses they were guiltless of wines and spirits. But the enormous price of 50*l*. per load suggested luxuries, and it was old Jonathan at The Idovers who introduced gin. Till then no gin even – nothing but ale – had been consumed in that far-away spot; but Jonathan brought in the gin, which speedily became popular. He called it 'spoon-drink' (a spoon being used with the sugar) as a distinguishing name, and as spoon-drink accordingly it was known. When anyone desired to reduce the strength of his glass, they did indeed pour him out some more water from the kettle; but having previously filled the kettle with the spirit, his last state became worse than the first.

While thus they revelled, the labourers worked with the flails in the barn threshing out the truly golden grain. The farmers used to take pains to slip round upon them unexpectedly, or meet them as they were going home from work, in order to check the pilfering of the wheat. The labourer was not paid wholly in cash; he had a bushel of the 'tail', or second flour, from the mill in lieu of money, settling once a month. Their life was hard indeed. But the great prosperity which had come upon the farmers did them no good. In too many cases it melted away in drink. The habit of drinking became settled in a family. Bad habits endured after the prosperity had departed; and in some cases those who had once owned their farms as well as occupied them had to quit the homes of their forefathers. Here and there one, however, laid the foundation of a fortune, as fortunes are understood in the country; and shrewd old Jonathan was one of these.

Even down to very recent days a spell of drinking – simple drinking – was the staple amusement of many an otherwise respectable farmer. Not many years since it was not unusual for some well-to-do farmer of the old school to ride off on his nag, and not be heard of for a week, till he was discovered at a distant roadside inn, where he had spent the interval in straightforward drinking. These habits are now happily extinct. It was in those old times that wheat was bought and hoarded with the express object of raising the price to famine pitch: a thing then sometimes practicable, though not always successful. Thus in 1801 the price of wheat in March was 55*l*. per load, while in October it had fallen to 15*l*. Men forgot the misery of the poor in their eagerness for guineas.

Hilary, with all his old prejudices, was not so foolish as to desire a return of times like that. He had undergone privation himself in youth, for farmers' sons were but a little better off than plough-lads even in his early days; and he did not wish to make money by another man's suffering. Still he was always grieving about the wheat crop, and how it had fallen in estimation. It was a sight to see the gusto with which he would run his hand into a sack of wheat to sample it. 'Here, feel this,' he would say to me, 'you can slip your hand in up to your elbow; and now hold up your palm – see, the grains are as plump as cherry-stones.'

After hearing Hilary talk so much of old Jonathan I thought I should like to see the place where he had lived, and later in the season walked up on the hills for that purpose. The stunted fir-trees on the Down gave so little shadow that I was glad to find a hawthorn under whose branches I could rest on the sward. The prevalent winds of winter sweeping without check along the open slope had bent the hawthorn before them, and the heat of the sultry summer day appeared the greater on that exposed height. On either hand hills succeeded to hills, and behind I knew they extended farther than the eye could reach. Immediately beneath in front there was a plain, at its extreme boundary a wood, and beyond that the horizon was lost in the summer haze. Wheat, barley, and oats – barley and wheat and beans, completely occupied the plain. It was one vast expanse of cereals, without a sign of human life; for the reaper had not yet commenced, and the bailiffs' cottages were hidden among the ricks. There was an utter silence at noonday; nothing but yellowing wheat beneath, the ramparts of the hills around, and the sun above.

But, though out of sight, there was a farmhouse behind a small copse and clump of elms full of rooks' nests, a short way from the foot of the Down. This was The Idovers, once the residence of old Jonathan; it was the last farm before reaching the hill district proper, and from the slope here all the fields of which it consisted were visible. The house was small, for in those days farmers did not look to live in villas, and till within the last few years even the parlour floor was of stone flags. Rushes used to be strewn in the halls of palaces in ancient times, and seventy years ago old Jonathan grew his own carpets.

The softest and best of the bean straw grown on the farm was selected and scattered on the floor of the sitting-rooms as warm and dry to the feet, and that was all the carpet in the house. Just before sheep-shearing time, too, Jonathan used to have the nettles cut that flourished round the back of the sheds, and strewn on the floor of the barn. The nettles shrivelled up dry, and the wool did not stick to them, but could be gathered easily.

With his own hands he would carry out a quart of beans to the pigs – just a quart at a time and no more, that they might eat every one and that none might be wasted. So, too, he would carry them a few acorns in his coat-pocket, and watch the relish with which the swine devoured their favourite food. He saved every bit of crooked wood that was found about the place; for at that date iron was expensive, and wood that had grown crooked and was therefore strong as well as curved was useful for a hundred purposes. Fastened to a wall, for instance, it did for a hook upon which to hang things. If an apple-tree died in the orchard it was cut out to form part of a plough and saved till wanted.

Jonathan's hard head withstood even the whirl of the days when corn was at famine prices. But these careful economies, this continual saving, put more money in his purse than all that sudden flush of prosperity. Every groat thus saved was as a nail driven into an oak, fixed and stable, becoming firmer as time went on. How strangely different the farmers of to-day, with a score of machines and appliances, with expensive feeding-stuffs, with well-furnished villas! Each one of Jonathan's beans in his quart mug, each one of the acorns in his pocket became a guinea.

Jonathan's hat was made to measure on his own special block by the hatter in Overboro' town, and it was so hard and stout that he could sit upon it without injury. His top-boots always hung near the fireplace, that they might not get mouldy; and he rode into market upon his 'short-tail horse', as he called his crop-tail nag. A farmer was nothing thought of unless he wore top-boots, which seem a distinguishing mark, as it were, of the equestrian order of agriculture.

But his shoes were made straight; not as now one to each foot – a right and left – but each exactly alike; and he changed his shoes every morning, wearing one on one foot one day and on the other the next, that they might not get worn to either foot in particular. Shoes lasted a great length of time in those days, the leather being all tanned with oak bark only, and thoroughly seasoned before it was cut up. There is even a story of a farmer who wore his best shoes every Sunday for seven years in Sundays – fifty years – and when he died had them buried with him, still far from worn out.

A traveller once returned from America – in those days a very far-off land – and was recounting the wonders he had seen, and among them how the folk there used sleighs, not only for driving in but for the removal of heavy goods. But Jonathan did not think it strange, since when he was young wheeled vehicles were not so common. He had himself seen loads of hay drawn home on 'sleds' from English meadows, and could tell where a 'sled' had last been used. There were aged men living about the hamlet in his day – if that could be called a hamlet in which there were barely a score of people, all told – who could recollect when the first waggon came to The Idovers. At all events, they pointed out a large field, called the Conigers, where it was taken to turn it round; for it was constructed in so primitive a style that the forewheels would not pass under the body, and thus required a whole field to turn in.

At that date folk had no banking accounts, but kept their coin in a strong chest under the bed, sometimes hiding it in strange places. Jonathan was once visiting a friend, and after they had hobnobbed a while the old fellow took him, with many precautions that they should not be observed, into the pig-sty and showed him fifty guineas hid in the thatch. That was by no means all his property, but the old fellow said, with a wink, that he liked to have a little hoard of his own that his wife knew nothing about.

Some land being put up for sale, after biddings by the well-to-do residents, an old dealer in a very small way, as was supposed, bid above them all. The company looked upon him with contempt, and his offer was regarded as mere folly; but he produced a nail-bag from under his coat and counted out the money. A nail-bag is made of the coarsest of all kinds of sacking. In this manner the former generation, eschewing outward show, collected their money coin by coin, till at last they became substantial men and owners of real estate. So few were the conveniences of life that men had often to leave the road and cross several fields out of their way to light their pipes at a burning couch-heap or lime-kiln.

They prided themselves then in that hill district that they had neither a cow nor a poor married man in the parish. There was no cow, because it was entirely a corn-growing place. The whole resident population was not much over a score, and of the labourers they boasted not one was married. For in those old times each parish kept its own poor, and consequently disliked an increase of the population. The farmers met in vestry from time to time to arrange for the support of the surplus labour; the appearance of a fresh family would have meant a fresh tax upon them. They regarded additional human beings as an incumbrance.

The millers sent their flour round the country then on pack-horses; waggons and carts were not so common as now, while the ways, when you once quitted the main road, were scarcely passable. Even the main roads were often in such a state that foot-passengers could not get along, but left the road and followed a footpath just inside the hedge. Such footpaths ran beside the roads for miles; here and there in country places a short section of such tracks may still be found. 'Pack-roads', too, may be occasionally met with, retaining their designation to this day. It was the time of the great wars with the First Napoleon; and the poor people, as the wheat went up to famine prices, were often in a strait for bread. When the miller's packhorse appeared the cottagers crowded round and demanded the price: if it had risen a penny, the infuriated mob of women would sometimes pull the miller's boy off the horse and duck him in the village pond.

The memory of those old times is still vivid in farmhouses, and at Hilary's I have myself handled old Jonathan's walking-staff, which he and his father before him used in traversing on foot those perilous roads. It was about five feet long, perhaps more, an inch and a half in diameter, and shod with an iron ferrule and stout spike. With this he could prod the sloughs and ascertain their depth, or use it as a leaping-pole; and if threatened by sturdy rogues whirl it about their heads as a quarter-staff.

Wars and famines were then terrible realities – men's minds were full of them, and superstition flourished. The foggers and shepherds saw signs in the sky and read the stars. Down at Lucketts' Place one winter's night, when folk almost fancied they could hear the roar of Napoleon's cannon, the old fogger came rushing in with the news that the armies could be seen fighting in the heavens. It was an aurora, the streamers shooting up towards the zenith, and great red spots among the stars, the ghastly stains of the wounded. The old fogger declared that as he went out with his lantern to attend to the cows calving he could see the blood dripping on the back of his hand as it fell down from the battling hosts above.

To us the ignorance even of such comparatively recent times is almost incredible. As Hilary was telling me of such things as we sat in his house one evening, there grew upon our ears a peculiar sound, a humming deep bass, somewhat resembling the low notes of a piano with a pressure on the pedal. It increased and became louder, coming from the road which passed the house; it was caused by a very large flock of sheep driven slowly. The individual 'baa' of each lamb was so mixed, as it were, with the bleat of its fellow that the swelling sound took a strange, mysterious tone; a voice that seemed to speak of trouble, and perplexity, and anxiety for rest. Hilary, as a farmer, must of course go out to see whose they were, and I went with him; but before he reached the garden gate he turned back, remarking, 'It's Johnson's flock; I know the tang of his tankards.' The flat-shaped bells hung on a sheep's neck are called tankards; and Hilary could distinguish one flock from another by the varying notes of their bells.

Reclining on the sweet short sward under the hawthorn on the Down I looked over the Idover plain, and thought of the olden times. As I gazed I presently observed, far away beside some ricks, the short black funnel of an engine, and made it out to be a steam-plough waiting till the corn should be garnered to tear up the stubble. How much meaning there lay in the presence of that black funnel! There were the same broad open fields, the same beautiful crops of golden wheat, the same green hills, and the same sun ripening the grain. But how strangely changed all human affairs since old Jonathan, in his straight-made shoes, with his pike-staff, and the acorns in his pocket, trudged along the footpaths!

Chapter VII.

The Cuckoo-Fields.

The cuckoos came so frequently to some grass-land just outside the Chace and sloping down to the brook that I gave the spot the name of the Cuckoo-fields. There were two detached copses in them of no great extent, and numerous oaks and hawthorns, while the brook below was bordered with willow-stoles. This stretch of grass was divided into two large fields by a line of decaying posts and rails, and it became a favourite resort of mine in the warm days of spring, because I could almost always see and hear the cuckoos there.

Why they should love it so much is not easy to tell, unless on account of the comparatively barren character of the soil. The earth seemed to be of a very different kind to that in the rich and fertile meadows and fields close by; for the grass was rough, short, and thin, and soon became greyish or brown as the summer advanced, burning or drying up under the sun. It may often be observed that a piece of waste, like furze, when in the midst of good land, is much frequented by all birds and animals, though where there is nothing else but waste they are often almost entirely absent.

As the oaks come out into full leaf, the time when the meadows become beautiful, the notes of the cuckoo sound like a voice crying 'Come hither' from the trees. Then, sitting on the grey and lichen-covered rail under the cover of a hawthorn, I saw sometimes two and sometimes three cuckoos following each other courting, now round the copse, now by the hedge or the brook, and presently along the rails where they constantly perched. Occasionally one would alight on the sward among the purple flowers of the meadow orchis. From the marshy meadow across the brook a peewit rose from time to time, uttering his plaintive call and wheeling to and fro on the wing. At the sound a second and a third appeared in succession, and after beating up and down for a few minutes settled again in the grass. The meadow might have been called a plovery – as we say rookery and heronry – for the green plovers or peewits always had several nests in it.

The course of the humble bees that went by could be watched for some way – their large size and darker colour made them visible – as they now went down into the grass, and now started forward again. The honey bees, small and somewhat lighter in colour, could not be seen so far. They were busy in the sunshine, for the hive bee must gather most of its honey before the end of July, before the scythe has laid the grass in the last meadow low. Few if any flowers come up after the scythe has gone over, except the white clover, which almost alone shows in the aftermath, or, as country people call it, the 'lattermath'. Near me a titlark every few minutes rose from the sward, and spreading his wings came down aslant, singing with all his might.

Some sarsen stones just showed above the grass: the old folk say that these boulders grow in size and increase in number. The fact is that in some soils the boulder protrudes more and more above the surface in the course of time, and others come into view that were once hidden; while in another place the turf rises, and they seem to slowly sink into the earth. The monotonous and yet pleasing cry of the peewits, the sweet titlark singing overhead, and the cuckoos flying round, filled the place with the magic charm of spring.

Coming to these Cuckoo-fields day after day, there was always something to interest me, either in the meadows themselves or on the way thither. The very dust of the road had something to show. For under the shadowy elms a little seed or grain had jolted down through the chinks in the bed of a passing waggon, and there the chaffinches and sparrows had congregated. As they moved to and fro they had left the marks of their feet in the thick white dust, so crossed and intertangled in a maze of tracks that no one could have designed so delicate and intricate a pattern. If it was cloudy, still, glancing over the cornfields, just as you turned partly round to look, there seemed a brilliant streak of sunshine across them. This was a broad band of charlock: its light yellow is so gaudy and glaring in the mass that as it first catches the eye it seems as if the land were lit up by the sun. After it the buttercups appear of a quiet colour, like dead gold in contrast.

Under-foot, almost in the very dust of the road, the silverweed opened its yellow petals, and where there was a dry bank, or by the gateways leading into the corn, the pink pimpernel grew. For some time I suspected the pimpernel of not invariably closing its petals before rain, and at last by precise observation found that it did not. Twice in a comparatively short period I noted the petals wide open within a few minutes of a shower. It appears rather to close during the atmospheric change which occurs previous to rain than to rain itself. Once now and then a shower seems to come up in the driest weather without warning or change in the atmosphere: the cloud is over and gone almost before it seems worth while to take shelter. To the approach of such shower-clouds the pimpernel does not invariably respond, but it is perfectly accurate if anything serious is brewing. By a furrow in the sward by the roadside there grew a little piece of some species of gorse – so small and delicate, with the tiniest yellow flowers, that it was well worthy of a place where it would be admired; for few could have seen it hidden there.

Birds'-foot lotus covered the sward of one part of the Cuckoo-fields, on the higher ground near the woods, where the soil was dry; and by the hedge there were some bushy plants of the rest-harrow, whose prickly branches repel cattle and whose appearance re-proaches the farmer for neglect. Yet though an outcast with animals and men, it bears a beautiful flower, butterfly-shaped and delicately tinted with pink. Now, as the days roll on, the blue succory and the scarlet poppies stand side by side in the yellow wheat but just outside my Cuckoo-fields, and one or two stray corncockles bloom; they are not common here and are perhaps brought from a distance. Here you may walk many miles and even wait several harvests to see a corncockle.

The thistledown floats; and see, yonder the white balls are rolling before the gentle air along the very tips of the bronzing wheat-ears. By the hedge the straggling stalks of St. John's wort lift the yellow petals dotted with black specks above the bunches of grass. The leaves, held up to the light, seem to have numerous eyelets, as if pricked but not quite through – windows in the leaf. In the grass the short selfheal shows; and, leaning over the gate, on the edge of the wheat you may see the curious prickly seed-vessels of the corn buttercup – the 'hedgehog' – whose spines, however, will not scratch the softest skin.

Resting on the rail under the hawthorn for a minute or two in early spring, when it was too chilly to stay long, I watched a flock of rooks and jackdaws soaring in the sky. Round and round and ever upwards they circled, the jackdaws of course betraying their presence by their call; up towards the blue, as if in the joy of their hearts, they held a festival, happy in the genial weather and the approach of the nesting-time. This soaring and wheeling is evidently done for recreation, like a dance. Presently the flock seems to tumble and fall, and there comes the rushing sound of the air swiftly parted by their outspread wings as they dive a hundred feet in a second. The noise is audible a quarter of a mile off. This, too, is play; for, catching themselves and regaining their balance just above the elms, they resume their steady flight onwards to distant feeding-grounds. Later in the season, sitting there in the warm evenings, I could hear the pheasants utter their peculiar roost-cry, and the noise of their wings as they flew up in the wood: the vibration is so loud that it might almost be described as thumping.

By-and-by the cuckoo began to lose his voice; he gurgled and gasped, and cried 'cuck – kuk – kwai – kash', and could not utter the soft, melodious 'oo'. The latest date on which I ever heard the cuckoo here, to be certain, was the day before St. Swithin, July 14, 1879. The nightingales, too, lose their sweet notes, but not their voices; they remain in the hedges long after their song has ceased. Passing by the hawthorn bushes up to the end of July, you may hear a bird within that seems to threaten you with a loud 'sweet-kurr', and, looking in, you will find it to be a nightingale. The spelling exactly represents the sound, the 'r' being twirled. 'Sweet-kurr-kurr' comes from the interior of the bushes with an angry emphasis.

Along the lower part of these meadows there was a brook, and the brook-sparrows were chattering ceaselessly as I walked among the willow-stoles by it one morning towards the end of June. On the left hand the deep stream flowed silently round its gentle curves, and on the other through the willows and alders the grassy slope of the Cuckoo-fields was visible. Broad leaves of the marsh marigold, the flower long since gone, covered the ground; light-green horsetails were dotted thickly about; and tall grasses flourished, rising to the knee. Dark shallow pools were so hidden under these grasses and plants that the presence of the black and yet clear water could not be perceived until the foot sank into it.

The sedge-birds kept just in front of me, now busy on a

willow-stole, and concealed in the grasses and moss which grew out of the decaying wood; now among the sedges covering the mudbanks where the brook had silted up; now in the hedge which divided the willows from the meadow. Still the peculiar sparrow-like note, the ringing chirp, came continually from their throats; the warm sultry day delighted them. One clung to the side of a slender flag, which scarcely seemed strong enough to support it, yet did not even bend under its weight; then on again as I came nearer – but only two or three yards – to recommence singing immediately.

Pushing through the brushwood and past the reddish willow-poles, I entered a very thicket of flags, rising to the shoulder. These were not ribbed or bayonet-shaped, but flat, like a long sword. Three or four sprang from a single root, broad and tall, and beside them a stalk, and on it the yellow iris in full flower. The marsh seemed lit up with these bright lamps of colour under the shadowy willows and the dark alders. There were a dozen at least within a few yards close around, and others dimly visible through the branches – three large yellow petals drooping, and on the curve of each brownish mottled markings or lines delicately stippled, beside them a rolled spike-like bloom not yet unfolded: a flower of the waters, crowned with gold, above the green dwellers by the shore.

Here the sedge-birds left me, doubling back to their favourite willow-stoles and sedges. Further on, the ground rose, and on the drier bank the 'gicks' grew shoulder high, towering over the brambles. It was difficult to move through the tangled underwood, so I went out into the Cuckoo-fields. Hilary had drained away much of the water that used to form a far larger marsh about here, and calculated his levellings in a most ingenious manner with a hollow 'gicks'. He took a wooden bowl, and filled it to the brim with water. Then cutting a dry 'gicks' so that it should be open at either end, like a tube, he floated it – the stalk is very light – on the bowl. Looking through this tube he could get his level almost as accurately as with an engineer's instrument, though of course it was more cumbrous to use.

There was a corner here that had not been mown for a long time, and in the autumn the wild carrots took possession of it, almost to the exclusion of grass and other plants. The flower of the wild carrot gathers together as the seeds mature, and forms a framework cup at the top of the stalk, like a bird's-nest. These 'bird's-nests', brown and weather-beaten, endured far into the winter. The brook-sparrows still sang as I passed by again in the evening; they seem the most unwearied of birds, for you may hear them all day, all the evening, and at one o'clock next morning; indeed, at intervals, all night. By night the note is, or appears to be, less sparrow-like, or perhaps the silence of night improves it to the ear. I stayed that evening in a corner of a wheatfield not yet yellow, and watched the shadows of the trees grow longer and broader as the sun declined.

As the breeze rushed over the corn there was a play of various shades of green, the stalks as they bent this and that way taking different hues. But under the the hedge it was still; the wind could not come through, though it moved the boughs above. A mass of cloud like flocks of wool, mottled and with small spaces of blue between, drifted slowly eastwards, and its last edge formed an arch over the western horizon, under which the sun shone. The yellow vetchling had climbed up from the ditch and opened its flower, and there were young nuts on the hazel bough. Far away in a copse a wood-pigeon called; nearer the blackbirds were whistling; a willow wren uttered his note high in the elm, and a distant yellowhammer sang to the sinking sun.

The brook had once been much wider, and in flood times rendered the Overboro' road almost impassable; for before a bridge was built it spread widely and crossed the highway – a rushing, though shallow, torrent fifty yards broad. The stumps of the willows that had grown by it could still be found in places, and now and then an ancient 'bullpoll' was washed up. This grass is so tough that the tufts or cushions it forms will last in water for fifty years, even when rooted up – decayed of course and black, but still distinguishable. In those times just previous to the construction of railways, when the lord of the manor came down after Parliament rose, there used to be a competition to get hold of his coachman. So few agricultural people travelled, and news came so slowly and in such distorted fashion, that the coachman became a great authority. Such a brook as this was then often a serious obstacle.

There was still an old punt, seldom used, to be found in a rickyard of Hilary's, close by which was an extensive pond. The punt was thatched over with flags from the stream. The moorhens were fond of this pond because it was surrounded with a great quantity of rushes; they were numerous all up the brook. These birds, being tame and common, are not much regarded either for sport or the table, yet a moorhen shot at the right time of the year – not till the frosts have begun – is delicious eating. If the bird were rare it would be thought to rival the woodcock; as it is, probably few people ever taste it. The path to Lucketts' Place from this rickyard passed a stone-quarry, where the excavated stone was built up in square heaps. In these heaps, in which there were many interstices and hollows, rabbits often sat out; and by stopping the entrance and carefully removing the stones they might occasionally be taken by hand. Next by the barn where in spring the sparrows made a continuous noise, chirping and quarrelling as they carried on their nesting operations: they sometimes flew up with long green bennets and grass fibres as well as with dry straws.

Then across the road, where the flint-heaps always put me in mind of young Aaron; for he once gravely assured me that they were the very best places in the world on which to rest or sleep. The flints were dry, and preserved the slumbering wayfarer from damp. He had no doubt proved this when the ale was too strong. At the house, as I passed through the courtyard, I found him just on the point of starting for Overboro' with a wallet, to bring back some goods from the shops. The wallet is almost unknown even in farmsteads now: it is a kind of long bag closed at each end, but with a slit in the centre for the insertion of the things to be conveyed. When filled it is slung over the shoulder, one end in front and the other behind, so as to balance. Without knowing the shape of a wallet the story of Jack the Giant-Killer stowing away such enormous quantities of pudding is scarcely to be understood: children nowadays never see such a thing. Many nursery tales contain allusions of this kind, the meaning of which must be obscure to the rising generation.

Within doors I found a great discussion going forward between Hilary and a farmer who had called, as to the exact relationship of a man who had just quitted his tenancy and another who died nearly forty years before. They could not agree either as to the kinship or the date; though the visitor was the more certain because he so well remembered that there was an extraordinary cut of 'turvin' that year. The 'turvin' is the hay made on the leaze, not the meadows, out of the rough grass and bennets left by the cows. To listen to the zest with which they entered into the minutest details of the family affairs of so long ago, concerning people with whom neither had any connection – how they recollected the smallest particulars – was astonishing. This marvellous capacity for gossip seemed like a revelation of a totally different state of society. The memory of country people for such details is beyond belief.

When the visitor left with his wife we walked to the gate and saw them down the road; and it was curious to note that they did not walk side by side. If you meet a farmer of the old style and his wife walking together, never do you see them arm-in-arm. The husband walks a yard or two in front, or else on the other side of the road; and this even when they are going to church.

Chapter VIII.

Cicely's Dairy.   Hilary's Talk.

Just outside the palings of the courtyard at Lucketts' Place, in front of the dairy, was a line of damson and plum trees standing in a narrow patch bordered by a miniature box-hedge. The thrushes were always searching about in this box, which was hardly high enough to hide them, for the snails which they found there. They broke the shells on the stone flags of the garden path adjacent, and were often so intently occupied in the box as to seem to fly up from under the very feet of any one who passed.

Under the damson tree the first white snowdrops came, and the crocuses, whose yellow petals often appeared over the snow, and presently the daffodils and the beautiful narcissus. There were cowslips and primroses, too, which the boys last year had planted upside down that they might come variegated. The earliest violet was gathered there, for the corner was enclosed on three sides, and somehow the sunshine fell more genially in that untrimmed spot than in formal gardens where it is courted. Against the house a pear was trained, and opened its white bloom the first of all: in its shelter the birds built their nests. The chaffinches called cheerfully on the plum-trees and sang in the early morning. When the apples bloomed, the goldfinches visited the same trees at least once a day.

A damask rose opened its single petals, the sweetest-scented of all the roses; there were a few strawberries under the wall of the house; by-and-by the pears above enlarged, and the damsons were coated with the bloom. On the tall plum-trees hung the large purplish-red plums: upon shaking the tree, one or two came down with a thud. The branches of the damsons depended so low, looking, as it were, right into the court and pressing the fruit against your very face as you entered, that you could not choose but take some when it was ripe. A blue-painted barrel-churn stood by the door; young Aaron turned it in the morning, while the finches called in the plum-trees, but now and then not all the strength of his sturdy shoulders nor patient hours of turning could 'fetch' the butter, for a witch had been busy.

Sometimes on entering the dairy in the familiar country way, you might find Cicely, now almost come to womanhood, at the cheese-tub. As she bent over it her rounded arms, bare nearly to the shoulder, were laved in the white milk. It must have been from the dairy that Poppæa learned to bathe in milk, for Cicely's arms shone white and smooth, with the gleam of a perfect skin. But Mrs. Luckett would never let her touch the salt, which will ruin the hands. Cicely, however, who would do something, turned the cheeses in the cheese-room alone. Taking one corner of the clean cloth in her teeth, in a second, by some dexterous sleight-of-hand, the heavy cheese was over, though ponderous enough to puzzle many a man, especially as it had to come over gently that the shape might not be injured.

She did it without the least perceptible exertion. At the moment of the turn, when the weight must have been felt, there was no knot of muscle visible on her arm. That is the difference; for

When Ajax strives some rock's vast weight to throw

the muscles of the man's limb knot themselves and stand out in bold relief. The smooth contour of Cicely's arm never varied. Mrs. Luckett, talking about cheese as we watched Cicely one morning, said people's taste had much altered; for she understood they were now fond of a foreign sort that was full of holes. The old saying was that bread should be full of holes, cheese should have none. Just then Hilary entered and completed the triad by adding that ale should make you see double.

So he called for the brown jug, and he and I had a glass. On my side of the jug stood a sportsman in breeches and gaiters, his gun presented, and ever in the act to fire: his dog pointed, and the birds were flying towards Hilary. Though rude in design the scene was true to nature and the times: from the buttons on the coat to the long barrel of the gun, the details were accurate and nothing improved to suit the artist's fancy. To me these old jugs and mugs and bowls have a deep and human interest, for you can seem to see and know the men who drank from them in the olden days.

Now a tall Worcester vasè, with all its elegance and gilding, though it may be valued at 5,000*l.*, lacks that sympathy, and may please the eye but does not touch the heart. For it has never shared in the jovial feast nor comforted the weary; the soul of man has never communicated to it some of its own subtle essence. But this hollow bowl whispers back the genial songs that were shouted over it a hundred years ago. On the ancient Grecian pottery, too, the hunter with his spear chases the boar or urges his hounds after the flying deer; the women are dancing, and you can almost hear the notes of the flute. These things were part of their daily life; these are no imaginary pictures of imaginary and impossible scenes: they are simply scenes in which every one then took part. So I think that the old English jugs and mugs and bowls are true art, with something of the antique classical spirit in them, for truly you can read the hearts of the folk for whom they were made. They have rendered the interpretation easy by writing their minds upon them: the motto, 'Prosperity to the Flock', for instance, is a good one still; and 'Drink fair; don't swear', is yet a very pleasant and suitable admonition.

As I looked at the jug, the cat coughed under the table. 'Ah,' said Mrs. Luckett, 'when the cat coughs, the cold goes through the house.' Hilary, returning to the subject of the cheese, said that the best was made when the herd grazed on old pastures: there was a pasture field of his which it was believed had been grazed for fully two hundred years. When he was a boy, the cheese folk made to keep at home for eating often became so hard that, unable to cut it, they were obliged to use a saw. Still longer ago, they used to despatch a special cheese to London in the road-waggon; it was made in thin vats (pronounced in the dairy 'vates'), was soft, and eaten with radishes. Another hard kind was oval-shaped, or like a pear; it was hung up in nets to mature, and traded to the West Indies.

He looked to see when the moon changed in 'Moore's Almanac', which was kept for ready reference on the mantelpiece. Next to Bible and Prayer-book comes old Moore's rubric in the farmhouse — that rubric which declares the 'vox stellarum'. There are old folk who still regret the amendments in the modern issue, and would have back again the table which laid down when the influence of the constellations was concentrated in each particular limb and portion of the body. In his oaken cabinet Hilary had 'Moore' from the beginning of the century, or farther back, for his fathers had saved them before him. On the narrow margins during his own time he had jotted down notes of remarkable weather and the events of the farm, and could tell you the very day cow 'Beauty' calved twenty years ago.

I thought the ale good, but Hilary was certain it was not equal to what he used to brew himself before he had so large an acreage to look after, and indeed before the old style of farm-life went out of fashion. Then he used to sit up all night watching – for brewing is a critical operation – and looking out of doors now and then to pass the long hours saw the changes of the sky, the constellations rising in succession one after the other, and felt the slight variations of the wind and of moisture or dryness in the air which predict the sunshine or the shower of the coming day. He seemed to have thought a good deal in those lonely watches; but he passed it off by referring to the malting. Barn barley was best for malting – *i.e.* that which had been stored in a barn and therefore kept perfectly dry, for ricks sometimes get wet before they can be thatched. But barn barley was not often come by nowadays, as one by one the old barns disappeared: burned, perhaps, and not rebuilt. He had ceased to brew for some time; Cicely could, however, remember sipping the sweet wort, which is almost too sweet for the palate after childhood.

They still baked a batch of bread occasionally, but not all that was required. Cicely superintended the baking, passing the barm through a sieve with a wisp of clean hay in it. The hay takes off any sourness, and ensures it being perfectly sweet. She knew when the oven was hot enough by the gauge-brick: this particular brick as the heat increased became spotted with white, and when it had turned quite white the oven was ready. The wood embers were raked out with the scraper, and the malkin, being wetted, cleaned out the ashes. 'Thee looks like a gurt malkin' is a common term of reproach among the poor folk – meaning a bunch of rags on the end of a stick. We went out to look at the oven; and then Mrs. Luckett made me taste her black-currant gin, which was very good. Presently we went into the orchard to look at the first apple-tree out in bloom. While there a magpie flew across the meadow, and as I watched it Mrs. Luckett advised me to turn my back and not to look too long in that direction. 'For', said she, 'one magpie is good luck, but two mean sorrow; and if you should see three – goodness! – something awful might happen!'[1]

One lovely June afternoon as Hilary and I strolled about the fields, we passed some lambs at play. 'Lamb is never good eating without sunshine,' said Hilary. Not only wheat and plants generally but animals also are affected by the absence of sun, so that the epicure should hope as devoutly as the farmer that the dull and overcast season of 1879 will not be repeated. Hilary's remark was founded upon the experience of long years – such experience as is only to be found in farmhouses where kindred succeed each other, and hand down practical observations from father to son.

The thistles were showing rather strongly in the barley – the result of last year's rain and the consequent impossibility of proper clearing. These thistles he thought came from portions of the root and not from seed. Last year all the farmers had been Latter Lammas men. The 1st of August is Lammas Day; and in the old time if a farmer had neglected his work and his haymaking was still unfinished on August 13 (*i.e.* old style), he was called in reproach a Latter Lammas man. But last year (1879) they were all alike, and the hay was about till September; yet Hilary could recollect it being all done by St. Swithin's, July 15.

Sometimes, however, the skilled and careful agriculturist did not succeed so well as the lazy one. Once in seven years there came a sloven's year, according to the old folk, when the sloven had a splendid crop of wheat and hardly knew where to put it. Such a harvest was as if a man had gone round his farm with the sun in one hand and the watering-pot in the other! Last year there had been nearly as much mathern (wild camomile) and willow-wind (convolvulus and buckwheat) as crop, and he did not want to see the colt's tail in the sky so often again. The colt's tail is a cloud with a bushy appearance like a ragged fringe, and portends rain.

I remarked that it was curious how thunderstorms sometimes returned on the same day of the week and at the same hour for a month running. Hilary said they had been known to return every day at the same hour. The most regular operation on a farm is the milking: one summer his fogger declared it came on to thunder day after day in the afternoon just as he took his yoke off his shoulders.

[1] see Notes page 115

Such heavy and continuous downpour not only laid the crops, but might spoil them altogether; for laid barley had been known to sprout there and then, and was of course totally spoiled. It was a mistake to associate thunder solely with hot weather; the old folk used to say that it was never too cold to thunder and never too warm to snow.

A sweet yet faintly pungent odour came on the light breeze over the next field – a scent like clover, but with a slight reminiscence of the bean-flower. It arose from the yellow flower of the hop-trefoil: honey sometimes has a flavour which resembles it. The hop-trefoil is a favourite crop for sheep, but Hilary said it was too soft for horses. The poppies were not yet out in the wheat. When in full bloom some of the cottagers gather the scarlet flowers in great quantities and from them make poppy wine. This liquor has a fine colour and is very heady, and those who make it seem to think much of it. Upon the hills where furze grows plentifully the flowers are also collected, and a dye extracted from them. Ribbons can thus be dyed a bright yellow, but it requires a large quantity of the flowers.

A little farther a sheep-dog looked at us from a gateway; and on coming nearer we found the shepherd busily engaged cutting the feet of his sheep one by one with a keen knife. They had got the foot-rot down in a meadow – they do not suffer from it on the arable uplands where folded – and the shepherd was now applying a caustic solution. Every shepherd has his own peculiar specific, which he believes to be the only certain remedy.

Tar is used in the sheepfold, just as it used to be when sweet Dowsabell went forth to gather honeysuckle and lady's-smock nearly three centuries since. For the shepherd with whom she fell in love carried

His tar-boxe on his broad belt hong.

So, too,

He leared his sheepe as he him list
When he would whistle in his fist;

and the shepherd still guides and encourages his sheep by whistling.

Hilary's Talk

Hilary said that years ago the dogs kept at farmhouses in that district did not seem of such good breeds, nor were there so many varieties as at present. They were mostly sheep-dogs, or mongrels of the sheep-dog cast; for little attention was paid to breed. Dogs of this kind, with shaggy black coats and stump tails, could be found at most farms, and were often of a savage disposition; so much so that it was occasionally necessary to break their teeth that they might not injure the sheep. From his description the dogs at the present day must be far superior; indeed, there seems to have been no variety of dog and no purity of breed at that time (in that neighbourhood); meaning, of course, outside the gamekeeper's kennels, or the hounds used for hunting. Shepherds like to keep their flock in hurdles, folded as much as possible, that they may not rub their wool off and so get a ragged appearance. Once now and then in wet weather the ground becomes so soft that a flock will not move, their narrow feet sinking so deeply in the mud. It is then necessary to 'dog them out' – to set the dog at them – and the excitement, fright, and exertion have been known to kill one or more of the flock.

Passing on to the lower grounds, we entered the meadows, where the men were at haycart. The cart-horses wore glittering brazen ornaments, crescent-shaped, in front of the neck, and one upon the forehead. Have these ornaments a history?[1] The carters and ploughmen have an old-world vocabulary of their own, saying 'toward' for anything near or leaning towards you, and 'vrammards' for the reverse. 'Heeld' or 'yeeld', again, is ploughman's language; when the newly sown corn does not 'heeld' or 'yeeld' it requires the harrow. In the next field, which the mowers had but just cut, the men were 'tedding' – *i.e.* spreading the swathe with their prongs. Hilary said that hay was a safe speculation if a man could afford to wait; for every few years it was sure to be extremely dear, so that the old people said, 'Old hay, old gold.'

As we returned towards Lucketts' Place, he pointed out to me a distant house upon which he said slates had been first used in that neighbourhood. Fifty or sixty years since no slates were to be seen there, and when they began to be introduced the old folk manifested great opposition. They said slate would never last – the moss would eat through it, and so cause holes; and, in fact, some of the slate that was brought up did decay and become useless. But that

[1] see Notes page 115

93

was, of course, an inferior kind, quite different to what is now employed. In so comparatively short a period has everything – even the mode of roofing – changed that the introduction of slates is still in many places within the memory of man. Hilary had still a lingering preference for thatch; and though he could not deny the utility of slate, his inclination was obviously in favour of straw. He assured me that good straw from a good harvest (for there was much difference in it), well laid on by a good thatcher, had been known to keep out the weather for forty-five years.

We looked into the garden at the Place, where Hilary particularly called my attention to the kidney-beans; for, said he, if the kidney-beans run up the sticks well, with a strong vine, then it would be a capital hop-year. On the contrary, if they were weak and poor, the hops would prove a failure. Thus the one plant was an index to the other, though they might be growing a hundred miles apart, both being particularly sensitive to the same atmospheric influences.

In a distant tree beyond the rickyard there was something hanging in the branches that I could not quite make out: it was a limb of a dead horse. A cart-horse belonging to a neighbouring farmer had met with an accident and had to be killed, when, according to old custom, portions were sent round to each adjacent farmstead for the dogs, which then had a feast. Thus, said Hilary, according to the old saw, the death of a horse is the life of a dog.

Chapter IX.

The Water-Mill. Field Names

'Our time be a-most gone by,' said the miller looking up from his work and laying aside the millpeck for a moment as he rubbed his eyes with his white and greasy sleeve. From a window of the old mill by Okebourne I was gazing over the plain green with rising wheat, where the titlarks were singing joyously in the sunshine. A millstone had been 'thrown off' on some full sacks – like cushions – and Tibbald, the miller, was dexterously pecking the grooves afresh.

The millpeck is a little tool like a double adze, or perhaps rather like two chisels set in the head of a mallet. Though age was stealing upon him, Tibbald's eye and hand were still true, and his rude sculpture was executed with curious precision. The grooves, which are the teeth of the millstone, radiate from the centre, but do not proceed direct to the edge: they slant slightly.

'There bean't many as can do this job,' he said, 'I can put in sixteen or twenty to the inch. These old French burrs be the best stone; they be hard, but they be mild and takes the peck well.' Ponderous as the millstones appear, they are capable of being set so that their surfaces shall grind with extreme accuracy. The nether, called the 'bed stone', is stationary; the upper millstone, or 'runner', revolves, and the grain crushed between the two works out along the furrows to the edge.

Now and then the miller feels the grain as it emerges with his pudgy thumb and finger, and knows by touch how the stones are grinding. It is perceptibly warm at the moment it issues forth, from the friction: yet the stones must not grind too close, or they 'kill' the wheat, which should be only just cracked, so as to skin well. To attain this end, first, the surfaces of the stones must be level, and the grooves must be exactly right; and, secondly, the upper stone must be hung at the exact distance above the other to the smallest fraction of an inch. The upper millstone is now sometimes balanced with lead, which Tibbald said was not the case of old.

'We used to have a good trade at this mill,' he continued, as he resumed his pecking; 'but our time be a-most gone by. We be too fur away up in these here Downs. There! Listen to he!' A faint hollow whistle came up over the plain, and I saw a long white cloud of steam miles away, swiftly gliding above the trees beneath which in the cutting the train was running.

'That be th' express. It be that there steam as have done for us. Everything got to go according to that there whistle: they sets the church clock by he. The big London mills as be driven by steam does the most of the work; and this here foreign wheat, as comes over in the steamers, puts the market down, so as we yent got a chance to buy up a lot and keep it till the price gets better. I seed in the paper as the rate is gone down a penny: the steamers be going to ship the American wheat a penny a bushel cheaper. So it bean't much good for Hilary to talk about his wheat. I thenks that'll about do.'

He laid down the millpeck, and took his millstaff to prove the work he had done. This was made of well-seasoned oak, two pieces put together so that they should not warp. He rubbed the edge with ruddle, and, placing the millstaff on the stone, turned it about on its shorter axis: where the ruddle left its red mark more pecking would be required. There was but one small spot, and this he quickly put right. Even the seasoned oak, however, is not always true, and to be certain on the point Tibbald had a millstaff prover. This is of rigid steel, and the staff is put on it; if any daylight is visible between the two the staff is not accurate – so delicately must these great stones be adjusted for successful grinding.

The largest of them are four feet two inches diameter; and dangerous things they are to move, for if the men do not all heave or 'give' at the same moment the stone may slip, and the edge will take off a row of fingers as clean as the guillotine. Tibbald, of course, had his joke about that part of the machinery which is called the 'damsel'. He was a righteous man enough as millers go, but your miller was always a bit of a knave; nor could he forbear from boasting to me how he had been half an hour too soon for Hilary last Overboro' market.

He said the vast water-wheel was of elm, but it would not last so long up so near the springs. Upon a river or brook the wheel might endure for thirty years, and grind corn for a generation. His millpond was close to the spring-head, and the spring-water ate into the wood and caused it to decay much quicker. The spokes used to be mortised in, now they used flanges, ironwork having almost destroyed the business of the ancient millwright. Of all manual workers, probably the old style of millwright employed the greatest variety of tools, and was the cleverest in handling them. There seemed no end to the number of his chisels and augers; some of the augers of immense size. In winter time the millwright made the millstones, for the best stones are not in one piece but composed of forty or fifty. The French burrs which Tibbald preferred come over in fragments, and these are carefully fitted together and stuck with plaster of Paris. Such work required great nicety: the old millwright was, in fact, a kind of artist in his handicraft.

I could not help regretting, as Tibbald dilated on these things, that the village millwright no longer existed; the care, the skill, the forethought, the sense of just proportion he exhibited quite took him out of the ranks of the mere workman. He was a master of his craft, and the mind he put into it made him an artist. Tibbald went on that he did not care for the Derby or Welsh millstones. These were in one piece, but they were too hard for the delicate grinding necessary to make the fine flour needed for good bread. They answered best for barley meal. Now, the French burr was not only hard but mild, and seemed to feel the corn as it crushed it. A sack of wheat lost 4 lb. in grinding. I asked about the toll: he showed me the old measure, reckoned at the tenth of a sack; it was a square box. When the lord's tenants in the olden times were forced to have their corn ground at the lord's mill, the toll was liable to be abused in a cruel manner; hence the universal opinion that a miller must be a knave. Even in much more recent times, when the labourers took part of their wages in flour, there is said to have been a great deal of sleight-of-hand in using the toll-box, and the miller's thumb grew fat by continually dipping into other folk's sacks.

But Tibbald had an argument even here, for he said that men nowadays never grew so strong as they used to do when they brought their own wheat to be ground at the mill, and when they made their bread and baked it at home. His own father once carried the fattest man in the parish on his back half a mile; I forget how much he weighed exactly, but it was something enormous, and the fat man, moreover, held a 56 lb. weight in each hand. He himself remembered when Hilary used to be the strongest man in the place; when the young men met together they contended who should lift the heaviest weight, and he had seen Hilary raise 5 cwt., fair lifting, with the hands only, and without any mechanical appliance. Hilary, too, used to write his name with a carpenter's flat cedar pencil on the whitewashed ceiling of the brewhouse, holding the while a ½ cwt. of iron hung on his little finger. The difficulty was to get the weight up, lifting it fairly from the ground; you could lift it very well half-way, but it was just when the arm was bent that the tug came to get it past the hip, after which it would go up comparatively easily.

Now this great strength was not the result of long and special training, or, indeed, of any training at all; it came naturally from outdoor life, outdoor work, plain living (chiefly bacon), and good bread baked at home. At the present time men ate the finest and whitest of bread, but there was no good in it. Folk grew tall and big – taller than they used to be, he thought – and they could run quick, and so forth; but there was no stamina, no power of endurance, of withstanding exposure like there was formerly. The mere measure of a man, he was certain, had nothing to do with his strength; and he could never understand how it was that the army folk would have men precisely so high and so many inches round. Just then he was called away to a carter who had brought up his team and waggon at the door, and as he was gone some time I went up under the roof, whence there was a beautiful view down over the plain.

The swifts, which had but just arrived, were rushing through the sky in their headlong way; they would build presently in the roof. The mill was built at the mouth of a coombe on the verge of the Downs; the coombe was narrow and steep, as if nature had begun a cutting with the view of tunnelling through the mass of the hills. At the upper end of the coombe the spring issued, and at the lower was the millpond. There is something peculiarly human in a mill – something that carries the mind backwards into the past, the days of crossbow and lance and armour. Possibly there was truth in Tibbald's idea that men grow larger in the present time without corresponding strength, for is it not on record that some at least of the armour preserved in collections will not fit those who have tried it on in recent times? Yet the knight for whom it was originally made, though less in stature and size, may have had much more vigour and power of endurance.

The ceaseless rains last year sent the farmers in some places to the local millers once more somewhat in the old style. Part of their wheat proved so poor that they could not sell it at market; and, rather than waste it, they had it ground at the village mills with the idea of consuming as much of the flour as possible at home. But the flour was so bad as to be uneatable. As I parted with Tibbald that morning he whispered to me, as he leaned over the hatch, to say a good word for him with Hilary about the throw of oak that was going on in one part of the Chace. 'If you was to speak to he, he could speak to the steward, and may be I could get a stick or two at a bargain' – with a wink. Tibbald did a little in buying and selling timber, and, indeed, in many other things. Pleased as he was to show me the mill, and to talk about it by the hour together, the shrewd old fellow still had an eye to business.

After a while, in walking along the footpaths of the meadows and by the woods, a feeling grew upon me that it would be pleasant to know something of their history. It was through inquiring about the age of the rookery that this thought took shape. No one could tell me how long the rooks had built there, nor were there any passing allusions in old papers to fix the date. There was no tradition of it among the oldest people; all they knew was that the rooks had always been there, and they seemed to indicate a belief that there the rooks would always remain. It seemed to me, however, that the site of their city was slowly travelling, and in a few generations might be found on the other side of the Chace. Some of the trees where the nests were most numerous were decaying, and several were already deserted. As the trees died, the rooks moved to the next clump, and thus gradually shifted their city.

This inquiry led to further reflections about the past of the woods and meadows. Besides the birds, the flowers, and animals that had been there for so many, many centuries, there were the folk in the scattered homesteads, whose ancestors might have left some record. In these times history is concerned only with great cities or strategical positions of world-wide renown; interest is concentrated on a siege of Paris or a march towards Constantinople. In days of yore battles were often fought in or near what seem to us mere villages; little places whose very names are uncertain and exact site unascertainable were the centres of strife. Some of these places are buried under the sward as completely as Herculaneum under the lava. The green turf covers them, the mower passes over with his scythe and knows not of them.

Hilary had observed in one of his meadows that the turf turned brown or burnt up in squares during hot summer weather. This he conjectured to be caused by the shallowness of the soil over some ancient foundations; and some years before he had had the curiosity to open a hole, and soon came upon a hidden wall. He did not excavate farther, but the old folk, when they heard of it, remembered a tradition of a village having once existed there. At present there were no houses near; the place, whatever it was, had disappeared. The mention of this meadow led to some conversation about the names of the fields, which are often very curious.

Such names as Lea, Leaze, Croft, and so on, are readily explained; but what was the original meaning of The Cossicles? Then there were Zacker's Hook, the Conigers, [1] Cheesecake, Hawkes, Rials, Purley, Strongbowls, Thrupp, Laines, Sannetts, Gaston, Wexils, Wernils, Glacemere, several Hams, Haddons and Weddingtons, Slades, and so on, and a Truelocks. These were quickly put down; scores of still more singular names might be collected in every parish. It is the meadows and pastures which usually bear these designations; the ploughed fields are often only known by their acreage, as the Ten Acre Piece, or the Twelve Acres. Some of them are undoubtedly the personal names of former owners. But in others ancient customs, allusions to traditions, fragments of history, or of languages now extinct, may survive.

There was a meadow where deep trenches could be traced, green now, but clearly once a moat, but there was not even a tradition about it. On the Downs overlooking The Idovers was an earthwork or entrenchment, of which no one knew anything. Hilary believed there was an old book – a history of Overboro' town – which might perhaps contain some information, but where it could be found he did not know. After some consideration, however, he thought there might be a copy at the Crown, once an old posting-inn, at Overboro': that was about the only place where I should be likely to find it. So one warm summer day I walked into Overboro', following a path over the Downs, whose short sward affords the best walking in the world.

[1] see Notes page 115

At the Crown, now no more an inn but an hotel, the archway was blocked up with two hand-trucks piled with trunks and portmanteaus, the property of commercial gentlemen and just about to be conveyed to the station. What with the ostler and the 'boots' and the errand-boys, all hanging about for their fees, it was a push to enter; and the waiters within seemed to equally occupy the passage, fetching the dust-coats and walking-sticks and flourishing coat-brushes. Seeing a door marked 'Coffee-room', I took refuge, and having ordered luncheon began to consider how I should open my subject with the landlord, who was clearly as much up to the requirements of modern life as if his house had been by a London terminus. Time-tables in gilt-stamped covers strewed the tables; wine lists stood on edge; a card of the local omnibus to the station was stuck up where all could see it; the daily papers hung over the arm of a cosy chair; the furniture was new; the whole place, it must be owned, extremely comfortable and the service good.

But it was town and not country – to-day and not the olden time; and I did not feel courage enough to ask for the book. I believe I should have left the place without mentioning it, but, fortunately looking round the room while the lunch was prepared, I found it in the bookcase, where there was a strange mixture of the modern and antique. I took down the history from between Rich's thin grey 'Ruins of Babylon' and a yellow-bound railway novel.

Towards the close of the eighteenth century a learned gentleman had taken much pains to gather together this account of the town. He began with the story of Brutus, and showed that one of the monarchs descended from the illustrious Trojan founded a city here. Some fossil shells, indeed, that had been dug up furnished him with conclusive proof that the Deluge had not left the site uncovered, since no how else could they have got there: an argument commonly accepted in his day. Thus he commenced, like the monks themselves, with the beginning of the world; but then came a wide gap down to Domesday Book. The hides and yardlands held by the conquerors – how much was in demesne, how many acres were wood and how many meadow – the number of servi, and what the mill paid were duly translated and recorded.

The descent of the manors through the monasteries and the persons who purchased them at the Dissolution filled several pages, and was supplemented with a charter recognising rights of infang and outfang, assize of bread and ale, and so forth. Finally, there was a list of the mayors, which some one had carried on in manuscript on a fly-leaf to within ten years of date. There was an air of precision in the exact sentences, and the writer garnished his tale with frequent quotations from Latin writers. In the midst was a woodcut of a plant having no sort of relevancy to the subject-matter, but for which he returned thanks for the loan of the block.

But he had totally omitted his own times. These quotations, these lists and charters, the extracts from Domesday, read dry and formal – curious, and yet not interesting. Had he described the squires and yeomen, the townspeople of his own day, their lives and manner of thinking, how invaluable and pleasing his work would have been!

Hilary said that in these little country towns years ago people had to be very careful how they acted, lest they should offend some local magnate. He remembered a tradesman telling him how once he had got into great disgrace for putting a new knocker on his private side door, without first asking permission and sending round to obtain the opinion of an old gentleman. This person had nothing whatever to do with the property, but lived retired and ruled his neighbours with a rod of iron. The old knocker was quite worn out, but the new one had scarcely been fastened on when the unfortunate owner was summoned to the presence of the irate old gentleman, who demanded with great wrath what on earth he meant by setting himself up above his station in this way. It was only by a humble answer, and by begging the old gentleman to walk down and look at the discarded knocker, promising that it should be replaced if he thought proper, that he could be appeased. A man then hardly dared appear in a new hat without first suggesting the idea to his social superior.

Chapter X.

The Coombe-Bottom. Conclusion.

'There is "two-o'clock bush"', said Cicely, pointing to a large hawthorn; 'the shepherds look from the corner of the entrenchment, and if the sun is over that bush they know it is two o'clock.' She was driving me in the pony-trap over the Downs, and we were going to call on Mrs. Luckett's brother, who had a farm among the hills. He had not been down to Luckett's Place for more than twelve months, and Cicely was resolved to make him promise to come. Though they may be in reality much attached and affectionate, country folk are apt to neglect even their nearest and dearest. The visit is put off from month to month; then comes the harvest, and nothing else can be thought of; and the longer the lapse the more difficult is the remedy. The footpath of friendship, says the ancient British triad, if not frequently travelled becomes overgrown with briars.

Those who live by the land forget the passage of the years. A year is but a harvest. After the ploughing and sowing and cleaning, the reaping and thatching and threshing, what is there left of the twelvemonth? It has gone like a day. Thus it is that a farmer talks of twenty years since as if it was only last week, and seems unable to grasp the flight of time till it is marked and emphasised by some exceptional occurrence. Cicely meant to wake her uncle from this slumber.

We started early on a beautiful July morning – partly to avoid the heat, and partly because Cicely wished to be away when young Aaron shortened the tails of the puppies in the rickyard. (This he did in the old-fashioned way, with his teeth.) Besides we thought that, if we waited till later, Uncle Bennet might be gone to market at Overboro'. We passed several farmers leaning or sitting on the stiles by the road, watching for a friend to come along and give them a lift into town. Some of them had waited like this every market morning for years. There were fewer on the road than usual, it being near harvest, when many do not so much care to leave home.

Upon reaching the foot of the Downs, Cicely left the highway and entered a narrow lane without hedges, but worn low between banks of chalk or white rubble. The track was cut up with ruts so deep that the bed of the pony-trap seemed almost to touch the ground. As we went rather slowly along this awkward place we could see the wild thyme growing on the bank at the side. Presently we got on the slope of the hill, and at the summit passed the entrenchment and the shepherds' timepiece. Thence our track ran along the ridge, on the short sweet turf, where there were few or no ruts, and these easily avoided on that broad open ground. The quick pony now put out his speed, and we raced along as smoothly as if the wheels were running on a carpet. Far below, to the right, stretched wheatfield after wheatfield in a plain between two ranges of the hills. Over the opposite slope, a mile away, came the shadows of the clouds – then down along the corn towards us. Stonechats started from the flints and low bushes as we went by; an old crow – it is always an old crow – rose hastily from behind a fence of withered thorn; and a magpie fluttered down the hill to the fields beneath, where was a flock of sheep. The breeze at this height made the sunshine pleasant.

Cicely said that once some snow lingered in the fosse of the entrenchment we had left behind till the haymaking. There was a snowstorm late in the spring, and a drift was formed in a hollow at the bottom of the fosse. The weather continued chilly (sometimes even in June it is chilly, and the flowers seem out of harmony with the temperature), and this drift, though of course it was reduced, did not melt but became consolidated like ice: a part still remained when the haymaking commenced. The pony now slackened his pace at a sharp ascent, and as he walked up we could hear the short song of the grasshoppers. There was a fir copse at the summit through which the track went; by the gateway as we entered there was a convolvulus out. Cicely regretted to see this sign that the sun had reached his greatest height: the tide of summer was full. Beyond the copse we descended by a deep-worn track into a 'coombe-bottom,' or valley, where were some cottages.

Cicely, who knew some of the old people, thought she would call, though most probably they would be away. We stopped at a garden-gate: it was open, but there was no one about. Cicely lifted the latch of the door to step in, country fashion, but it was locked; and, hearing the noise, a cat came mewing round the corner. As if they had started out of the ground, a brown-faced boy and a thin girl suddenly appeared, having come through the hedge.

'Thaay be up to barken' (rickyard), said the boy: so we went on to the next door. It was locked too, but the key was in the lock outside. Cicely said that was a signal to callers that the wife had only gone out for a few minutes and would return soon. The children had followed us.

'Where is she?' asked Cicely.

'Hur be gone to dipping-place,' replied the boy. We went to a third door, and immediately he cried out, 'Thuck's our feyther's: the kay's in the thatch.' We looked and could see the handle of the key sticking out of the eave over the door.

'Where are they all?' I said.

'Aw, Bill's in the clauver; and Joe – he's in th' turmuts; and Jack be at public, a' spose; and Bob's wi' the osses; and – '

'They will be home to luncheon?' said Cicely.

'Aw, no um wunt; they wunt be whoam afore night; thaay got thur nuncheon wi' um.'

'Is there no one at home in all the place?' I inquired.

'Mebbe Farmer Bennet. Thur beant nobody in these yer housen.'

So we went on to Uncle Bennet's, whose house was hidden by a clump of elms farther down the coombe. There were cottagers in this lonely hill hamlet, not only old folk but young persons, who had never seen a train. They had not had the enterprise or curiosity to walk into Overboro' for the purpose. Some of the folk ate snails, the common brown shell-snail found in the hedges. It has been observed that children who eat snails are often remarkably plump. The method of cooking is to place the snail in its shell on the bar of a grate, like a chestnut. And well-educated people have been known, even in these days, to use the snail as an external medicine for weakly children: rubbed into the back or limb, the substance of the snail is believed to possess strengthening virtues.[1]

We found Uncle Bennet just taking his lunch in the stone-

[1] see Notes page 115

flagged sitting-room, which, however, had a square of cocoa-nut matting. He was getting on in years, but very active. He welcomed us warmly: still I thought I detected some uneasiness in his manner. His conscience warned him that Cicely was going to attack him for his remissness; and how was he to defend himself?

Without any preliminary, she at once demanded why he had not come down to see them.

'Mary', said he, calling the servant, as if he did not hear her, 'Some ale, and the ginger wine, and the grey-beard – mebbe you'd like a drop a' shart' – to me; but I declined. She repeated her question, but Uncle Bennet was looking towards me.

'The wuts be very forrard,' said he, 'I got some a-most ready to cut.'

'Do you hear?' cried Cicely, angrily.

'Niece,' replied the farmer, turning to her, 'there's them summer apples as you used to like, there be some ready; will 'ee have one?'

'I don't want your apples; why didn't you come down?'

'Aw; that's what you be a-talking about.'

'Yes, that's it.'

'The turmots wants some rain terrable bad' (to me) – 'you med see the fly a-hopping about 'em.'

'I hope they will spoil your turnips,' said Cicely; 'you are a very rude man not to answer a lady when she speaks to you.'

'You be a-coming on nicely, Cissy,' said he. 'Have 'ee got are a gage-ring yet?'

'How dare you!' (blushing). 'Tell me instantly why have you not been to see us? You know how angry it makes me.'

'Well, I was a-coming,' deliberately.

'When were you coming?'

'Well, I got to see a man down your way, Cissy; a' owes me for a load a' straw.'

'Then why don't you come down and get the money?'

'I told 'ee I was a-coming. He wants some of our sheep to feed off a meadow; s'pose I must see about it' – with a sigh, as if the idea of a decision was insupportable.

'Why didn't you come before?'

'Aw, I don't seem to have no time' – farmers having more time than anybody else.

'You could have come in June.'

'Bless 'ee, your feyther's got the hay about; a' don't want no strangers bothering.'

'As if you were a stranger! Well, why didn't you come in May?'

'Lor bless 'ee, my dear.'

'In April?'

'Us was main busy a-hoeing.'

'In March?'

'I had the rheumatism bad in March.'

'Well, then,' concluded Cicely,'now just change your coat and come to-day. Jump up in the pony-trap – we will make room.'

'To-day!' in hopeless bewilderment, his breath quite taken away at the idea of such sudden action. 'Couldn't do't – couldn't do't. Got to go down to Thirty Acre Corner: got to get out the reaping machine – a' wants oiling, a' reckon; got some new hurdles coming; 'spects a chap to call about them lambs;' a farmer can always find a score of reasons for doing nothing.

'All rubbish!' cried Cicely, smiling.

'Nieces be main peart now-a-days,' said he, shutting one eye and keeping it closed, as much as to say – I won't be driven. Then to me, 'There won't be many at market to-day.'

'I am hungry,' said Cicely softly; 'I should like some bread and honey.'

'Aw; should 'ee?' in gentler tones; 'I'll get 'ee some: will 'ee have it in th' comb? I got a bit left.'

She knew his pride in his bees and his honey; hill farmers still keep large stocks. He brought her a slice of home-baked bread and a piece of comb. She took the comb in her white fingers, and pressed the liquid gold from the cells; the luscious sweetness gathered from a thousand flowers making her lips still sweeter. Uncle Bennet offered me a jar full to the brim: 'Dip your vinger in,' said he.

'Why is the honey of the hills so much nicer?' asked Cicely, well knowing, but drawing him on.

'It be th' clover and th' thyme, and summat in the air. There bean't no hedges for um to fly up against, and so um carries home a bigger load.'

'How many hives have you?' I inquired.

'Let's see' – he counted them up, touching a finger for each twenty – 'there be three score and sixteen; I have a' had six score years ago, but folk don't care for honey now sugar be so cheap.'

'Let us go and see them,' said Cicely. We went out and looked at the hives; they were all in a row, each protected by large 'pansherds' from heavy rain, and placed along beneath the wall of the garden, which sheltered them on one side. Uncle Bennet chatted pleasantly about his bees for an hour, and would, I believe, have gossiped all day, notwithstanding that he had so little time for anything. Nothing more was said about the delayed visit, but just as we were on the point of departure, and Cicely had already taken the reins, he said to her, as if it were an afterthought, 'Tell your mother, I s'pose I must look down that way next week.'

We passed swiftly through the little hamlet; the children had gathered by a gateway to watch us. Though so far from the world, they were not altogether without a spice of the impudence of the city arab. A tall and portly gentleman from town once chanced to visit this 'coombe-bottom' on business, and strolled down the 'street' in all the glory of shining boots, large gold watch-chain, black coat and high hat, all the pomp of Regent-street; doubtless imagining that his grandeur astonished the rustics. A brown young rascal, however, looking him up – he was a tall man – with an air of intelligent criticism, audibly remarked, 'Hum! He be very well up to his ankles – and then a' falls off!'

That evening was one of the most beautiful I remember. We all sat in the garden at Lucketts' Place till ten o'clock; it was still light and it seemed impossible to go indoors. There was a seat under a sycamore tree with honeysuckle climbing over the bars of the back; the spot was near the orchard, but on slightly higher ground. From our feet the meadow sloped down to the distant brook, the murmur of whose stream as it fell over a bay could be just heard. Northwards the stars were pale, the sun seems so little below the horizon there that the glow of the sunset and the glow of the dawn nearly meet. But southwards shone the dull red star of summer – Antares, seen while the wheat ripens and the ruddy and golden tints come upon the fruits. Then nightly describing a low curve he looks down upon the white shimmering corn, and carries the mind away to the burning sands and palms of the far south. In the light and colour and brilliance of an English summer we sometimes seem very near those tropical lands.

So still was it that we heard an apple fall in the orchard, thud on the sward, blighted perhaps and ripe before its time. Under the trees as the months went on there would rise heaps of the windfalls collected there to wait for the cider-mill. The mill was the property of two or three of the village folk, a small band of adventurers now grown old, who every autumn went round from farm to farm grinding the produce of the various orchards. They sometimes poured a quantity of the acid juice into the mill to sharpen it, as cutting a lemon will sharpen a knife. The great press, with its unwieldy screw and levers, squeezed the liquor from the cut-up apples in the horsehair bags: a cumbersome apparatus, but not without interest; for surely so rude an engine must date back far in the past. The old fellows who brought it and put it up with slow deliberative motions were far, far past the joy with which all the children about the farm hailed its arrival. With grave faces and indifferent manner they ground the apples, and departed as slowly and deliberately as they came; verily men of the autumn, harbingers of the fall of the year.

As I dreamed with the honeysuckle over my shoulder, and Antares southwards, Hilary talked at intervals about his wheat as usual and the weather, but I only caught fragments of it. All the signs were propitious, and as it had been a fine harvest under similar conditions before, people said it would be fine this time. But, unlike the law, the weather acknowledged no precedent, and nobody could tell, though folk now thought they knew everything. How all things had changed since the Queen ascended the throne! Not long since Hilary was talking with a labourer, an elderly man, who went to the feast in Overboro' town on the day of the coronation. The feast was held in the market-place, and the puddings, said the old fellow regretfully, were so big they were brought in on hand-barrows.

It was difficult since he himself remembered even to learn the state of the markets. So few newspapers came into country places that before service on Sundays the farmers gathered round anybody in the churchyard who was known to take in a paper, to get particulars from this fortunate individual. Letters rarely came to the farmhouse door then. The old postman made a very good thing of his office – people were so eager for news, and it was easy to take a magpie glance at a newspaper. So he called at the butcher's before he started out, and in exchange for a peep at the paper got a little bit of griskin, or a chop, and at the farmhouses as he passed they gave him a few eggs, and at the inns a drop of gin. Thus a dozen at least read scraps before it reached the rightful owner.

If anything very extraordinary had happened he would shout it out as he went through the hamlet. Hilary said he well remembered being up on the roof of the house one morning, mending the thatch, when suddenly a voice – it was the postman's – cried from the road, 'Royal Exchange burned down!' In this way news got about before the present facilities were afforded. But some of the old folk still regretted the change and believed that we should some day be punished for our worship of steam. Steam had brought us to rely on foreign countries for our corn, and a day would come when through a war, or a failure of the crops there, the vast population of this country would be in danger of famine. But 'old folk' are prone to prophesy disaster and failure of all kinds.

Mrs. Luckett chimed in here, and said that modern ways were not all improvements, the girls now were so fond of gadding about. This was a hint for Cicely, who loved a change, and yet was deeply attached to the old home. She rose at this, doubtless pouting, but it was too dusky to see, and went indoors, and presently from the open window came the notes of her piano. As she played I dreamed again, till presently Mrs. Luckett began to argue with Hilary that the shrubs about the garden ought to be cut and trimmed. Hilary said he liked to see the shrubs and the trees growing freely; he objected to cut and trim them. 'For,' said he, 'God made nothing tidy.' Just then Cicely called us to supper.

NOTES

The following interesting correspondence has been received.

MAGPIE OMENS *Page* 91. – In reference to the superstition that one magpie is good luck, but two sorrow, 'R.F.' writes from Wiesbaden: – 'In the north of England the contrary belief holds good, witness the following saw which I heard many years ago in the county of Durham:-

"One for sorrow, two for mirth;
Three for a marriage, four a birth;
Five for heaven, six for hell,
Seven – the devil's own sel!"

As to seventeen, which number I once saw together, Mrs. Luckett's exclamation "Goodness! something awful might happen" might have been appropriate: only nothing dreadful did occur.'

CART-HORSE ORNAMENTS *Page* 93. – As to the history of the crescent-shaped ornaments on carthorses, 'J.D.' writes from Dover: 'Anyone who has lived in Spanish countries must be struck on going to East Kent by the gay trappings of the farmers' horses on gala days, in which the national colours of Spain, scarlet and orange yellow, and the "glittering brazen" ornament of the crescent and the cross, so generally prevail. Their history must date from the introduction of the Flemish breed of horses to this country, showing that as the Moors carried the crescent to Spain, so the Spaniards took it to Flanders, and the Flemings here, whence it has been adopted pretty generally by the farmers of England.'

NAMES OF FIELDS *Page* 102. – 'The Conigers is evidently the same as Coningar, a word sometimes occurring in Scottish local nomenclature, and which meant a rabbit-warren – Coniger, Coney-garth. I know two Coningars in Aberdeenshire, but the meaning of the word is as much forgotten there also. -H.W.L.'

MEDICINAL USE OF SNAILS *Page* 109. – In Dorset, writes 'S.C.S.S.,' an extract of snails for external use is still sometimes prepared and, mixed with rum, is rubbed into weak backs, or legs, especially of children.

GLOSSARY

barm	yeast, fermenting agent
bombarrel	bumbarrel, the long-tailed tit
brook-sparrow	sedge warbler
bull-poll	the tufted hair-grass, *Deschampsia cespitosa*
burr-stone	a siliceous rock
butter-and-eggs	toadflax, *Linaria vulgaris*
caddle	disturb, upset
corn buttercup	*ranunculus arvensis*
damsel	an iron rod with projecting pins, whose purpose is to shake the hopper, the box that delivers the grain to the millstones
dibbling machine	to dibble is to make holes in the earth for sowing
effet	newt or small lizard, eft
fogger	a cowman or keeper of cows
gallus	('gallows' as adverb) very, extremely
gicks	more usually kex, the dry, hollow stem of cow parsley, etc.
griskin	a lean part of loin, usually of a pig
honey-bottle	the cross-leaved heath, *Erica tetralix*
honey-plant	plant especially favoured by bees; furze or gorse
hop trefoil	*Trifolium campestre*
Idovers	Draycot Foliat, near Chiseldon
infang	infangthief, the right of a lord of a manor to try and punish a thief caught within its bounds. Outfangthief allowed him to pursue the thief outside its bounds.
loppet	to run with heavy gait, as a hare – by extension, an idler
moll-hern	heron
moon-daisy	the ox-eye, *Chrysanthemum leucanthemum*
mugwort	*Artemisia vulgaris*
moucher (moocher)	someone who picks up a country living as he can, not an honest workman. To mooch had a strong special sense of picking blackberries, as by schoolboys playing truant from school.
nuncheon	a drink or snack taken between main meals – by extension, luncheon

Okebourne	Chiseldon, four miles south-east of Swindon
Overboro'	Marlborough, some twelve miles south of Swindon
pansherd	a piece of broken earthenware pan
patten	a wooden-soled shoe
pin-wire	wire from which pins are made
prong	pitchfork
ruddle	red ochre, as used for marking sheep
sarsen	a very hard sandstone, found in boulders on the Wiltshire downs
skit	a slight shower
square	honest, straightforward
tric-trac	an old version of backgammon
turmuts	turnips
uck	to remove firmly, to heave out. Perhaps from the old dialect word 'hoke', to wound with horns, to gore
vox stellarum	'the voice of the stars'
vrammards	fromwards, away from
wallows	raked up lines of hay before cocking
wort	unfermented beer. Sweetwort was before the addition of hops
wurrut	wart
wuts, wurts	oats
yarbs	herbs

John Fowles, author of *The Magus, The French Lieutenant's Woman, Daniel Martin, A Maggot*, etc., has long been interested in nature and man's attitude to it, the subject of his essay *The Tree*. He has long admired Richard Jefferies' writings, and in 1980 introduced his novel *After London* in the OUP World Classics series. He lives in Dorset, and is honorary curator of the Lyme Regis Museum.

Graham Arnold moved to Devizes, Wiltshire in 1974 to devote himself full-time to drawing and painting. He derives much inspiration from the downland landscape which Richard Jefferies so enjoyed, and was a founder member of the Brotherhood of Ruralists group of artists. He now divides his time between Shropshire, where he recently settled, and Devizes, where he maintains a studio.

Other Wiltshire related titles include:

CURIOUS WILTSHIRE by Mary Delorme

In this original and substantial work, historian and author Mary Delorme
presents in-depth studies of six features of Wiltshire which contribute
much to the uniqueness of the county: Water Meadows, White Horses,
Sarsen Stones, Dew Ponds, Blind Houses and Tithe Barns.

The well researched and expertly written text is complemented by some
60 specially commissioned black and white photographs which illustrate
aspects of *Curious Wiltshire* visible today.　　　160 pages　Price £4.95

TOURING GUIDE TO WILTSHIRE VILLAGES
by Margaret Wilson

'This voyage of discovery will take you to some of the loveliest villages
England has to offer'; so says the author in her Introduction to this inviting
and practical guide to rural Wiltshire.

Margaret Wilson has explored the length and breadth of the County;
her detailed descriptions are intriguingly interwoven with the human
stories associated with particular places.

Fully illustrated with line drawings and maps.　　　160 pages　£3.95

The above books may be obtained from your local bookshop or from the
publisher, post-free, at 1 The Shambles, Bradford on Avon, Wiltshire.
A current list of titles will be sent upon request.